Brilliant Disguises: Antique Love Songs for the Boss: 1978-1995

by

Ms. Jennifer Jazz

DORRANCE
PUBLISHING CO
EST. 1920
PITTSBURGH, PENNSYLVANIA 15238

Dorrance Publishing Co
585 Alpha Drive
Suite 103
Pittsburgh, PA 15238
Visit our website at *www.dorrancebookstore.com*

ISBN: 978-1-6480-4085-6
eISBN: 978-1-6480-4897-5

Epitaph

In memory of the person I was, until I could no longer write:

I've come this far, alone at the wheel no one can know the great engine I feel no one can realize the work that's gone in to making this motor turn over again. – Jennifer Jazz

the lord is my shepherd
i cannot sleep
he opened my eyes
and it all looked so cheap
he gave me a kingdom
that i cannot touch
until every mouth
is filled with too much

the lord is my shepherd
he gave me harsh words
regardless of my actions
i can never be his nurd
free from the arrows
you toss my way
the lord is my shepherd
he taught me how to play...

he makes me hang out
on the beach when i can
i learned long ago
to sacrifice who i am
the words may rub
and the acts may grind

but nothing matters except
which way you draw the line

the lord is my shepherd
those things are in the past
today is a new year
it's easy to lose your grasp
of the point i'm making
don't take my game for real
even your own soft body
will one day lose its feel

the lord is my Shepherd
i'm the woman at the well
and everyone passes judgment
on when i'll be sent to hell
but the lord is my Shepherd
i'm all she will ever be
harlot, angel, woman
crucified on some dude's tree

you're wrapped up in a catalog
a bible in one hand
a fast guitar, a bank account
you're the clean-cut American man
and i sit in my window

i see the things you do
you've no respect for broken wings
when the final act comes due

i never think about it
those things i say to you
i use myself to help you see
just what a person will do
all i care about
is the side you make your stand
whether it is black or white
you're a front-page rock-'n-roll man

you point at me
and look at you
so perfect
in repose
no mistakes, no sinner you
in dry-cleaned silkened clothes
the lord—he is my shepherd
i lean upon his staff
and watch the sheep begin to
baaahhhhh
as i feed them with my laugh.

there's a man i've loved so long
and i hold him close each night
but it's just in dreams that i get him alone
and he leaves with the morning light
oh, i know he'd make me feel better
he's promised me that he'll try
to open up his woman's soul
and never fill it with lies

> take me in my blue satin nightgown
> and i don't mind if it tears
> and you can have these white silk stockings
> take away all my cares

i got a boy shinin' like silver
swingin' my heart like a stone
it makes a path skippin' over the river
where he's gonna give me a home
...a home, some flowers and joy in the sunshine
i might even learn to make bread
takin' a bath at sunset together
and i'll always beat him to bed

he can take me in my blue satin nightgown
and i won't mind if it tears
and hey, throw away those soft silk stockings
this lady don't even care

i understand what you're talkin' about
the way you want things to be
come to me, baby, and never let go
i need all your lovin' in me
put me down for paradise
someplace i know we can find
holding my dreams up to the window
leavin' my sorrows behind

oh, take me in my blue satin nightgown
i don't even mind if it tears
and honey, you can run those white
silk stockings
you take away all my cares...

what if we try
and don't make it
what if we don't
and never know
yearning my life away
like a puppet in the wrong play
i never knew
i'd let my feelings show

drivin' down the street
you're on the radio
tellin' me you'll love me
from now on
and baby, what am i gonna do
but bring it on home to you
drivin' down the street
listenin' to your song

what if we try
and don't make it
what if we don't
and never know
i go to sleep each night

prayin' god will make it all right
you're far away and honey
the days move slow

i know my past looks bad
but i was tryin'
to find my way from the darkness
to the light
what can anybody say
when i'd give you the rest of my days
gotta give it a chance
hey, this time
it's gonna be all right

what if we try
and don't make it
and honey, what if we don't
and never know
my love grows more each day
i'm the puppet in my own play
and whatever this thing is
i can't let go

what if we try and don't make it
what if we don't and never know

i'd give my life away

and there's nothin' anybody can say

i'm in love, i can't help it if my feelings show...

no, i don't have a man
and i live right down the road
won't ya follow me on home tonight
help me carry my load

follow me on home tonight, now
follow me on home tonight
no, i ain't feelin' right now, baby
i ain't feelin' right
and put your shoes out on the front
porch, darlin'
i know you'll need a little light
just follow me on home tonight, baby
follow me on home tonight

it's a long and sad story
i know you know it well
i come from around these parts, baby
there ain't a thing to tell
i spend my life weary
no, i don't have a dime
my tires got no tread on 'em
the engine's got no time

(CHORUS)

there's a baby in the bedroom
there's clothes still on the line
and sometimes i walk around outside
i see folks who look so fine
they shine like silver dollars
their hands are full of rings
and me, i sit on the front porch, baby
that's where i'm the king

(CHORUS)

could you hold me in your arms tonight
can i sleep up close to you
i won't say a word, i won't make a fuss
if you'll hold me, honey, i get so blue
i can fix you grits for breakfast
you can shower when it's the dawn
'cause i know you're the type to move on, darlin'
but will you hold me till you're gone

and follow me on home tonight
please follow me on home tonight

no, i'm not feelin' right, sweet baby
i'm not feelin' right
and put your arms around me
you know i try, with all my might
just follow me on home now, baby
follow me on home tonight

DANCE PARTNERS TONIGHT

i've read my book six times
finished my chores for the day
made enough money to pay the bills
there's no duty stuck in my way

the tree-frogs are goin' off
the cats have been fed
autumn moves closer
as i lie down in bed

and that's all i've had
for months at a time
each day repetitive
i don't realize i'm blind

to everything offered
that doesn't ring true
but when i think of you here
well, there's nothin' i'd
rather do...

CHORUS:

come here, step close, babe
we can dance on the deck
the crickets are yellin'
they're sayin', "what-th'-heck!"
it's been a long time
since we moved in starlight
press up close to me, darlin'
dance partners tonight

i waited so long for
a man on a horse
somebody fine now
a hero, of course
two-steppin' together
i can whistle a'tune
press up close to me, baby
we can dance 'neath the moon

lovers are creatures
exploring new highs
the end of the story
where the well soon runs dry
tho' the odds appear that
they'll never succeed

you can tell just by lookin'
(at 'em)
lovers their own speed

CHORUS:

So come and step close now
we'll dance on the deck
the tree-frogs are mating
maybe you'll gnaw on my neck
it's been a long time since
you've held me real tight
press up close to me, baby
dance partners tonight...

HIGH LANDS...

i first noticed it
when they barred the door
let me in for my fix
but there wasn't any more
none for me
& plenty for them
seems that the times
have changed again

my dancin' shoes
are still tucked away
for the last big party
doomsday
i watch them too
people who need to be
entertained
in the blink of an eye
none remain

my heart started out
in the meadows & hills
Riding my pony
unaware of the thrill
sucked into their game
& squashed like a bug
i feel a lot better now
swept under the rug

this world has stolen
our youth and our kids
took our good dreams
& tightened the lid
each man for himself
or each man saves us all
i'm right there beside you
in case you should fall

we knew back then
what it is today
we knew there'd be moments
we wouldn't wanna stay
the doomed generation
or witnesses born
of our freedom & lessons

generations scorned

drape your arm,
cross my shoulder now
join with me, dancin'
Laughin' out loud
come to the party
an open door
there is a way out
you so back in for more

lay out your cards
but your fortune on me
a gamble for rascals
you get what you see
each man a hero
and all of us saints
a Roll of the dice
it is what it ain't

i wouldn't trade places
with anyone else
who else could make sense of
what i find in myself
these must be the last days

we heard prophesized
just hold me close, man
Whisper your lullabies

goodbye illusion
goodbye gettin' fooled
Goodbye war & suffering
goodbye to their rule;
I welcome a new law
the one we let slip by
we have the chance now
to break the tie.

PAID IN FULL

when i stand before you
your child who finished up
emptied all the dishes
and washed out all the cups
they can never stand and deny me
i came thru like a bull
i ran that extra mile for you
and paid my bill in full

I'm paid in full
you can stop the song 'n dance
i walked across the waters raging
sometimes i took a chance
no one can deny me
i'm cornered, like an ornery bull
i bit the head off of the beast
and paid my bill in full

paid in full
you can leave my stuff at the door

i'm ready to go on, now
i've evened up the score
when you're handin' out silver lockets
and trinkets to the winner of the game
i'll be in front, with my hand outstretched
ready to give my name

paid in full
i'm a free-wheelin' sucker for a show
wonderin' what you've got there, hidden
wonderin' how fast it can go
paid in full
i got here just in time
to catch the last set of the night
played to a tune that's mine...

I THOUGHT YOU WERE ALL GROWN-UPS

most folks don't do
big deals every day
they get up, do laundry
solve obstacles in the way
living out their own drama
then run home to hide
and wonder why their guts
keep burning inside

i thought everyone participated
in this world
everyone was in on
a secret
something only grown-ups
passed among themselves
and a controlling power
unrelinquished

maybe people feel
as lost as i do
traveling alone in
this desert;
lookin' for a swimming pool
out on the interstate
something this suffering
might merit

if you've got it
you stand to lose
if you move around a bit
even like a young girl
at a truckstop
and all the caution
won't hold back the winds
once they're blowin' up
cross the prairie

where is your kindness
and where is your honor
where has your heart
slowly gone
none of you are building
together for your friends

and we'll watch the skies

reclaim

what it comes after.

SADDLE UP 'N RIDE OUT

when all my days
have come to this
sleeping on the floor
with no one to kiss
looking back at
people walking by
i miss you, baby
no matter what else i try

ever the loner
with bad haircut days
tossed aside
with no place to stay
haunted by evil
that caws in my ear
i miss you, baby
and why aren't you here

    ever the husband
    the father, the man

who walks with his honor
as part of his stand
he's still my hero
and i'm still alone
i miss you, baby
...someday they'll be grown

it's gone on so long now
i could stop and throw up
the love stuck inside me
my cross and my cup
ever the lovers
'til death do us part
i miss you, baby
you're the beat of my heart

if this was the finale of
the story of my self
i'd call it a day now
and go someplace else
but i hope there's a rainbow
in the valley 'round the bend
i'll wait a little longer
and join my love again

i have this romeo
he's the best dude in town
always keeps lookin' at
my good side when i'm down
someday we'll ride out
together in the sun:
for the end of this story of
how the west was won.

IF IT WASN'T FOR YOU

the only thing good
about my days on this earth
is the voice that you gave me
and what our treasures
are worth

if it wasn't for you
i'd be a sad, sad song
buried in a box
        in my room
        'til i'm gone

when i look back over
the time i let slip by
i tell a sad story
and not an eye is dry

you're given one chance
and you're lucky to get that
when it's gone

you still have years
to wonder
where it's at

you watch the presents
bestowed on you
        withdraw
and you stand and see
the humble figure
broken from the fall
and you wanted so much
and you tried so hard
but the baseball wasn't gonna go
and land inside your yard

it's a waste of time
to look upon the past
and when there's only a few grains left
to go
within your hourglass
you stand up tall
and let another game
        begin

if it wasn't for you, boss
i would have
thrown the towel in...

(IT WAS) ...SUNG BY A BIG FAT BABE

thru all the years
along all the roads
the fantasy i've lived for
has gone into overload
the same old tune
sung by a woman, fat:
        "somewhere is my lover..."
i wanted it to
        be like that

and always illusive
she goes giggling
down the path
leaving me speechless
and incurring her whip-wrath
"give me my lover!"
i'd cry out loud
and my fantasy would snicker
and turn away, proud

i have lived with a harsh
cruel mistress
all the days of my life;
i begged for my lover
and i wound up somebody's wife
today i sit here, lonely
forgotten...by the sea
and i never had my lover
waiting at home for me

i've pushed aside obsessions
(writing books and drawing fish)
important things would wait until
my lover was my wish
but now the time is over
the years have slipped away
and left me here alone, forsaken
        no lover waits today

and nothing was completed
no stories written well
my life went by without me
while i waited for her bell;
the tinkling of her windchimes
just outside my door

the vision of someone to love
        you know, i really expected
        more.

there was never a succinct person
who stayed with me each night
year in, year out, and played with
what i now know was my fright
that same old tune
was sung by a big fat babe
fooled me all my life
and made me her slave

i was looking for a man
but he never appeared
it must have been a fantasy
and it played
        right here
there's nothing else i wanted
nothing could catch my eye
and now, i'd better look elsewhere
because that moment
        passed me by

and i sit here like a sailor
accursed, for his sea
landlocked forevermore
no one to fish with me
arms outstretched, enchanted
i run giggling, in my hat
the bitch has made me speechless
and i wanted it
to be like that

i know there's nothing you
wouldn't do for me
whether i'm fifty years old
or just twenty-three
though we can't be together
we're never apart
i live my life, darlin'
you live my heart

they say i'm getting older
i tend to forget
the beach is still wild here
just like when we met

i keep comin' back to
where it all got a start
and let my days roll by
'cause you caught my heart

feel like i know
interstate 75
like i know what you're thinkin'
and how far you'll drive

no one can take away
the love on our part
i live my life, darlin'
you live my heart

my little girl's grown up
your kids are just born
babe, i know those highways
my shoes are still worn
and what remains
is my soft breath in the dark
somehow i go on
but you left your mark

i've done everything
i was sent out to do
applause for a broken man
baby, my best for you

tears fallin' now
where the ocean tears apart:
i live my life, darlin'
you live my heart.

DRIVE-BY ROMANCE

well, you know i never see you
(you're) always in your limousines
hiding behind gangsta windows
...it's been a long cold dream

and a drive-by romance
this must be LA style
safe sex from a distance, babe
i can't take another mile

of this drive-by romance
my baby's in a car
and it's a drive-by romance
i really don't know who you are

i've needed you beside me
you know you turn this engine on
first ya need to unlock The Club, babe
before my steering wheel's wrong

it's a drive-by romance
and i've been sayin' it for so long
begging for your sweet touch, babe
before the love's all gone

it's a deadly drive-by looting
he's married now with kids
and he's hiding behind windows
has my sweet babboo hit the skids

a drive-by romance
in a fast-food take-out car
moves along like a dino, baby
i just don't know where we are

am i just another drive-by romance
get me from a fast-food chain
my drive-by romance
this girl will never be the same

he checks out my pad
he checks out my job
he checks me out at night, well
i'm the girl he even tried to rob

it's a drive-by romance
i love a california man
and it's a drive-by looting
sometimes i don't know where i stand

in this drive-by romance
he's protected in his car
from the wild woman in me
honey, won't you tell me
        where we are

SOMEWHERE THERE'S A PARADISE

we don't know each other
but i know you'll be here soon
you sure took your time
in comin' 'round
to my room;
your name's been on my lips
before i even left home
i knew you were out here
waitin' for me
your name was somethin'
        i've known:

and somewhere there's a paradise
full of flowers and cats
miles of pounding oceans
and people who wear hip hats
somewhere there's a place for me
i know i've found my spot:
i live for you in paradise
full of what life's not

i saw you from my window:
it was a beautiful view
hair like miles of asphalt
laid out for me, it's true
everything about you
held mystery on the stage
a boy who was a king alone
hey, you left me crazed

and somewhere there's a paradise
full of stars that shine
miles of rocks that calm me down
and secret places all mine
somewhere there's a place for me
i think i've found my home
i live for you in paradise
it's something i've always known

come home with me, baby
sleep over in my arms
i know there's other girls out there
but none who have my charms
nothin' very fancy

it's a simple point of view
makes me sweat just picturing
what the two of us would do

'cause somewhere there's a paradise
with houses in neat rows
miles of black and gold oceans
and people who wear cool clothes
somewhere there's a place for me
i've waited for this so long
i live for you in paradise
and everything else has gone.

On a full-moon-summer's evening
I SAT UP, ON THE EMERALD COAST
AND THOUGHT ABOUT MY OLD WHITE COAT
I WORE THAT NIGHT YOU PLAYED "HOST"...
TO A SOLD-OUT 8-NIGHT CONCERT
IN LA. - BY - THE - SEA
WHEN I WAS JUST
ANOTHER RUNAWAY WIFE
OH, DO YOU REMEMBER ME?

IN LAVENDER SOX, WHITE CORD PANTS
I WAS DRESSED TO THRILL OR MISS,
I PICKED OUT THOSE CINNAMON SLINGBACKS
HOW COULD ANYONE ELSE Resist?

AND I WAS STILL A GIRL.
I LAID OUT IN THE SUN EACH DAY
WORKING ON MY CALIFORNIA TAN
HOPING NOTHING COULD GET IN MY WAY.

NOW I'VE COME FULL CIRCLE.
DOWN 'N DIRTY I RAN

& I WOUND UP IN MISSISSIPPI
OH, WHY CAN'T YOU UNDERSTAND...

THE TEASER IN THE WINDOW
THE WINDOWPANES FORM A JAIL
AROUND THE DREAMS
IN MY WHITE COAT POCKETS
RIPS & TEARS IN MY SAIL

THE DIME STORE CLERK, SHE WAVERS
TRYING TO FIGURE OUT WHO'S BOSS
WHICH ONE HOLDS THE KEY TO UNLOCK
THE UNICORN BOX I LOST

YOU KNOW, IT SEEMS PRETTY SCARY
MASQUERADING AROUND TOWN AS A NERD
HIDING THE DIAMONDS
LACED THRU MY HAIR
AND CHOKING BACK ALL THE WORDS

HE LIVES IN A MANSION ON THE HILLSIDE
WITH HIS SECOND WIFE POISED IN THE DOOR
AND TONITE, AS MY HUSBAND SLEEPS BESIDE ME
I'D BE WILLING TO RUN BACK FOR MORE

I COULD GET BACK HOME, TO MY BELOVED

THERE'S AN AIRPORT BUS EARLY TO LA

I KNOW I CAN BE THERE IF I HURRY

BY SUN-UP, I COULD BE HOME

IN ONE DAY

i was cooking myself some dinner
and suddenly, you were on tv
stroking your guitar in the kitchen
somethin' about a valentine
        for me.

i dried my hands
and turned up the tv
leaned in
        to see what i could see:
you and some guy were there
        singin'
        about a valentine
        a dark night
        and me.

i thought about your baby
i thought about your girl
i remembered that photo
        in your doorway with them
        and the past came by
        and gave me a whirl...

today, i am a new man
a housewife in the sink
bathrobe and sox
    on friday night
    you know, this line could rhyme
    with "stink."

but you were sayin'
    valentine
    it echoed 'round the room
and i stood there;
    with my stuffed-up nose
    like a bride caught out of tune

somethin' 'bout a valentine
what month is this, it's march
how could this be
    a song of mine
    and my throat closed up there,
    parched

well, what was that on tv
when i came home late from work
somethin' about a valentine
just another quirk

oh, let me be your valentine
(i could) hum it right along
sounded like a love song there
...back where i belong

oh, won't you be my valentine
i would from it with your song
it's been awhile since we "did it" again
wonder if i would follow along...

but let me be your valentine
i could hang out on tv
for the folks out there
        on friday night
to see what they could see...

if you didn't love me
and if the market didn't rise
i wouldn't go on living
butting my horns
        in your eyes.

suffering thru these lessons
(don't they know i'm made to play!)
if you didn't love me, baby
it would end my days

i live this life deadpan
a finger to all you folks!
i wasn't made to argue
and laugh politely at jokes
i wasn't made to wallow
in shit—well, not for long
i'm here for the good times, baby
a chance to audition my song

if you didn't love me
and if you slowly turned away

there'd be no more makin' fun of this
it would be the end to my days

i live to catch you sideways
slipping down the alley tonight
i'm here for just a quickie, even
anything you do is all right
if you didn't give me your attention
none of the pain would make sense
you're the shooting star in my eyes, baby
my tomcat on the fence

so if you didn't love me
and if money was all you made
i'd bury these bones in a bucket, baby
the end to this charade

there's more to this story
than rock-'n-roll
more than raising kids and bail
more than another girl on your arm
this story's become an epic tale
you're the breath inside of me
you're the louisiana road in the mist

you're the blood and guts and my old guitar
you're the boy i've yet to kiss

if you didn't love me, baby
if the creek don't rise
there'd never be another day in my life
with me there's no compromise

when i needed you
you weren't around
when there was nobody else
you were nowhere to be found

i'll remember
long past this time;
when i needed someone
you refused to be mine

i sit stroking
the city at night, wandering around
like a moth
trying to light
tearful
sometimes a bit lost
when i needed you, baby
it was too high a cost

and i'll remember
long past this time
my face in your pillow
the scent of your kind

i'll remember
how you turned your back
i may love you tonight
but i'll remember
        your act.

moments
sweep past us like sand:
i'll remember you, baby
i'll remember
        my hunger
        for the man....

...now, take a look
at the landscape below:
see the things we're shrugging off
stretched in the distance...
...this is the meaning, as you
reach for my hand:
i'll wait for you long nights
with no resistance

what could i offer
to an angel sent below?
how 'bout a bowl of candy, baby
something we both know
songs that come much closer
than any dream-come-true
this is what i offer, baby
i give my world to you

CHORUS:
the road to bowls of candy
mornings full of sun
days spent shaking sand out, baby
a life that's just begun

a life with you in paradise
it's all i care to see
another day of wonder, baby
that you fulfill for me

it's a vision full of windows
i sit in the sun
looking past the window-glass
at how this world is run
no place for these homeless souls
strangers who are lost
people in my window-glass
as i survey their cost

love paid for in shoelaces
tied up in big bows
it's a world that shoves you
to your knees
with nowhere left to go
no warm nights
no candleflame
just sorrow comin' down
this is what i offer you
i'll turn your world around.

(CHORUS)

let's go to the ocean, baby, let's swim with the tide,
let's paddle out on surfboards, baby, i'll take you for
a ride, where neptune guards the heroes and sun
gods turn tonight, this is what i offer, baby,
someplace to make it right

i was born a poor child
but i got rich as i grew
towering over other school kids, baby
growing up for you
and tho people often look at me
as a square peg in a round hole
this is what i offer, baby
a chance to reach your soul...

on the road to bowls of candy
days drenched full of sun
days spent shaking sand out, baby
my life just begun
making you in paradise
is all i wanna see
it would be like seeing a rainbow, baby
a dream-come-true for me.

i look at you
thru silent visions
old days move aside
for those of heftier meaning
        remove from me those hours
        when memories turn to confront
        even the more stoic
        of our children

my life begins with the motion
of sorrow swept away
along brightly lit paths
of leftover evenings
spent paying off these dues
        often i lay down
        in the blissful state
        of circumstance
        and plead to my creator
        to change this cup
        to a glass

the scorekeeper has no respect
for other tender excuses

the eye upon the donut
demands no second glance
        and me, i bide this time
        along another wretched highway
        coming upon an adventure
        sent to appease my mistrust

and i will have the last laugh
as you gaze at my dust
with wonder
on roads you've never heard about
in places you don't go
        for i put her thru her paces
        flying on to another victory
        i'll meet you there someday
        when you catch up to the
        scorekeeping dude

when you think of me
when you're older
in your rocking chair
on the porch
remember me as a rascal
who ran wild
while igniting a torch

i got what i went after
and it couldn't be had
with bucks
i'm king of my own mountain
and all the rest of it
sucks.

i have this thing about the highway
the rush of another new town
memories crowding out my good sense
and it's time to turn around
i get into my car
i get behind the wheel
when i get on the highway, babe
all i want's a good deal.

CHORUS:
that's just the way it happens, babe
that's just the road I'm on
the highway is my Lullaby
i don't know no other song
one road leads to pleasure
another road leads to pain
when I am in the middle
it's time to hit the road again

if you stand on the highway
and hitch a ride with me
you know I need the best life
that's the way it's got to be

tears and salty sorrow
are left there in the bend
I ease into the next town, babe
And I'm on my way again

CHORUS:
That's just the way it happens, babe
That's just the road I'm on
The highway is my lullaby
It never does me no wrong
One road leads to pleasure
And the other road always rains
When bad things come into my life
I turn and hit the road again

If we take this romance
With us for a little ways
You know I'll thank the stars above
For bringin' me brighter days
This life is a prison
Where right things turn out wrong
I'm ready for a good time, babe
If you wanna come along

CHORUS:

that's just the way it happened to me

that's just the road i'm on

the highway is my lullaby

I always seem to get along

One road brings me happiness

The past just brings me pain

When I am on the highway, babe

I'm glad to be gone again...

i didn't know
i went head-over-heels about you
caught off-guard
you slipped inside so fast
and all the precious moments
passed between us
i want the kind of love
that's built to last.

i know it broke your heart
        to read that letter.
you wondered how i could
        become so crass
unaware the sorrow
        tucked within me
i thought, like dreams at night
        my hurt would pass

i fell in love:
i wonder if i know the meaning
of what we do together
        in the night
it's important that i learn

about your feeling
as we make our way entwined
toward the light

you're a good man,
someone i'd wanna marry
a person i could tell
my troubles to
i'm ashamed to find these ghosts
there lurking
by the time i find them all,
i won't find you

i know i've not grown up
will you forgive me
i make some big mistakes
i travel fast
all the pain and silence
there inside me show me
that i need
to leave my past

you've been my great white hero
on a pony
this great romancer

    how i love you near!
and me, i run so quick
often i falter
when someone touches all
    those things so dear

trapped within the canyons
    of my daydreams
flicker silhouettes
    along the hall
i rush in nightgowns
    thrilled against your shadow
maybe you'll be home
    next time i call.....

happy birthday, baby
i'm hung up, it's true
how can i swear my love to somebody
when all i'm wantin' is you

when, for years, i'm glued to my radio
for messages somehow about us
and every guy i get where i want
i blow them off like dust

you married somebody else.
you didn't wanna know me.
gee, baby, i don't blame you.
i know there's not much here
        for you to see

and i'm leanin' hard on the time
taking it all in stride
40 years old and still hopin'
for my baby
        and my one good ride.

it's sad, even to me.
that i love you this much
        but it's true.
and somewhere, somehow, one day, baby
this love's gonna go and find you.

i'll live my life uncommitted
to anyone else on this earth
i myself could never tell some guy
hey, you are the one that it's worth.

i guess i was born to love.
and that's just the way
        that it lies.
every day you're married to her
is another goddamn day that i die.

is this what you wanted to hear?
i hope you're doin' okay
i'll be all right—whatever you want, baby,
my life just goes on this a'way.

it's another day of dreams
clutched against my chest
another day of windows
my heart don't get no rest
another day of mourning
alas, my life has gone
another day without you
and i barely get along

save those kisses for me
i'm so close to you now
and hold our love tightly
and promise that somehow
we'll always stay together
no matter what tomorrow brings
swear i'll be your angel
and you will be my king

no, you never make it
i'm alone on down this trail
the winds are full of arrows
the thunder in my sails
a moment full of blessing

a night beside your charms
i swear i love you, baby
take me back there in your arms

ponies fill my daydreams
and children fill these days
i wonder, is there a soldier
set out to come my way
another kindred spirit
who's weary from the war
is there somebody out there
for me...this, lord, i swore

to be his special angel
clothed now in garments white
and i'll hold him high above me
standing in the shiny light
i'll be his honey-darlin'
before the dark moves in
and steals us to another world
where we all live in sin

oh, i'd give you hundreds
in gold, if i had won
the battle on this long road

without having to turn and run
just to pass the hours
curled in my secret place
with the man who disappears
and leaves without a trace

save your kisses for me
i'm so close to you now
and hold our souls together
make it easier somehow
to reach out and remember
the joy that love can bring
swear i'll be your angel
and you will be my king

my expectations too high
my bedroom nights are low
i asked too much
        from a wild young man
        who has too many places to go

gone are the days
i find
long nights
        slip past my window
gone are the days
long nights
and no place else to go
long nights
he pushed my love away
long nights
slip past me every day

baby, please
you know nothin' else means more
(come back here)
than your knocking on my door
what else is my life for?

(you're so dear
baby, come back here)
you've made my heart so sore

baby, come back here
you know i love you
i need you near
baby, you're so dear
filled with too much fear
long nights
no place i wanna go
you made my world move slow
with things i don't wanna know

i guess i expected things too high
made my love run dry
and no place else to go
it's so slow
there's nothin' else i wanna know

she'll never take you there
she knows not of my place
even tho you love it so much
and it fills up all
        your singing-space

she looks so much like you
her bones, her hair, her skin
maybe she's your soulmate
baby, true love to do you in

they say she'll carry your fame
with class—and your money too
you fell for fifty-dollar workouts, baby
mine would have been free for you

let him go...let him go
i hear everyone say
i never knew i could hate you so much
as i did on your wedding day

i'm still four certificates ahead of you
it's a record that's hard to surpass

a bunch of silly mistakes back there
smudges on the window-glass

they're predicting the dow to fall to 1,000
they must put little faith in my drive
for whenever i write love songs for you, babe
the love lives on
'til i'm no longer alive

i've seen all my boyfriends marry
i've been thru all their breakups too
and i've learned one thing about these sojourns,
baby
my boyfriends always return...it's true

i will never forsake the home we've made
a place where our children can nest
with pride, i am beside you at night
i know you did your best

and all the family adores you
you've seen throngs as you went here & there
these are my rock star's sons & daughters
i think we've always made a good pair

this girl that you have married
will never share our bed
she may question you of the rumors, baby
but i'll always go over her head

no one loves you like i do
i'll carry it with me to my grave
i'll be waiting here by the window-box, baby
i'll take care of the dream we made,

So there you are
With your model affair
A lump in my throat
And mousse in my hair

We've come to this
I am really amazed
That the love of my life
Gone and left me crazed

A bone of contention
You sit on my mind
And all the things you didn't do
Start up the old grind

And do you say that of me
That you're glad it's gone
The way you felt is over
And you're coming on strong

Where do you keep
All the things I wrote

Have you thrown them all away
Did you give up hope

Or are you too busy
With all your pearls
All my life, you know
I'm gonna be your girl

You never stopped to thank me
You never shook my hand
You never gave me
What you give
To any other man

Much less model women
Who sit hungry at your feet
You never held me
Long and close
Until I fell asleep

I marvel at your direction
You took me for what you could
You never even done your part
You took me down real good

There's no divorce
No introduction
Or parties on the way
So this is how you chose to act
You really know how
To make my day

The rest of my life
Will be afterthoughts
Of all the life we missed (I missed)
The beach
The bedroom
And all the little kids
Baby, I am pissed

I watch you on the tv
I turn the channel;
        When you sing in the car
No matter how many
Boys are around
My heart's gonna be
With my rock-'n-roll star

At least you had a hit record.
If it had flopped I'd have

dropped my jeans
And you never ever realize
What it is
To breathe life into dreams

I know what you're thinking:
I've got it all and I don't
Have to pay
Don't have to listen
To that redneck bitch
I don't have to let her
Ever get her way

You've made my life
Worse than it was
At least I was dumb
About men:
I thought that I could
Bring it to me
But baby
I was wrong again

I've become the silent observer
I observe the lady you have
And every night I toss so hard

Feelin' real sad

Batted about like a cotton ball

I pray my soul to take

For I have died

One thousand times

And I can't get myself awake

i've watched the things
that meant so much to me,
turn and run
like a child lost
alone in the forest
seeking out the sun
for tho the love i held
to me
like painted glass
now shatters in the aftermath
i know
this too will pass...

i carried you close
thru the warm summer nights
and thru the winter i called you
come home, let's get right—
tho you never heard
and you never reached out
you'll always be the boy
i sit and dream about

you're right when you say
your work is better than you;
i never knew a boy could make
a little girl so blue
we had the chance
for so much, now
you've crushed it hard
with your feet
i never knew the dreams could die
or turn so bittersweet

may the women you hold
and the children they bear
never be a bit like me
and never really take you there
may your days ahead
be as bad as mine behind
you're a real disappointment, baby
god knows, you are resigned

and when the road ahead
looks like the road behind
remember i'll be waiting there
to give you a piece of my mind
no matter what, baby

my love

pops it in gear

down the road:

wish you weren't so shallow, baby

more of a prince

than a toad.

where is my son?
where has he gone?
he's not here, mom—
your son's not along

what's that you say—
what do you mean?
where is my son, child
the son in my dream?

you never had him.
he never came down.
he's still out there waiting
for his dad to come 'round

and you lost your mind
(it's been many years)
the man you loved so much
never turned back the tears

where is my son...
now where has that boy gone

i know i raised him
        up right
and they say he's not along
what do they know
i'm in my own space
with the man that i love
written wild across my face

where is my son?
where has he gone?
he's not come here
tho it's been so long

who would keep
my children from me
the same coldhearted man
who tied me to a tree
left me to die
in the cool desert night
left me counting
the stars across my sight

where is my son?
i've lost my mind
praying for my children

the ones i cannot find
who would deny
this light in my heart
the beam for the child
who cannot play his part—

his father doesn't want him
doesn't want our family
man turns his back on his boy
that's no man to me

where is my son?
you mean
i've waited all this time
to hold my little boy
and all i got was rhyme??

where is my son?
i feel him close to me.
but his father's too busy
doesn't want what
i can see.

you took my son
away from me

lost in the thunder
of other people's families
when you're an old man
you'll regret your choice
you'll be alone without us all
but you'll still have your voice
go on—croon to your audience
but we will not be there
our father was too busy
to show us that he cared
our dad was busy peeking out
and didn't have the time
to share me at the altar
and make the little boy mine.

Psalm 37:37

i know, from all the things you say
that somewhere in your heart
stands a man
who's really okay

but questions turn around
my mind
i wonder what it is with you
that makes you so unkind

  i look at other women
  protected by their man
  somebody there
  to help them out
  it's a life i'll never understand

  what keeps you so far from me
  i watch you from this glass
  who have you held
  all winter long
  to make the coldness pass

who sleeps right there beside you
a woman
with her man
it's a strange, lost feeling
i get from you
it's a feeling i'll never understand

you've never had to suffer
go hungry thru the night
you've never gotten up each day
to curse the morning light

every moment you leave me
out here to fend alone
is another day i curse your name
until the love has gone

you know i don't want your money
i only wanted...the man.
to help me live thru this nightmare
to deal with these things
i'll never understand

you deny me the treasures
that cost nothing on this earth

you hold yourself away from me
what is your game really worth?

i find the never-ending story
no way to get any peace
and every night i close my eyes
and pray for the bad dream release

It's a cement summer
for me
no sandy beaches with fun
it's a hot city day alone, babe
you know i sure do
need me someone

don't you ever think about me
don't you wonder who keeps
the motor on
it's not a real man
who turns these wheels
it's a plastic record
you can sing along

it's a sad, sad time of year
when my fishtail sits on dry land
when i finish school
and trade in my car
i'm on A1A
to find the dream man

who are you holding tonight
do you ever pretend she's me
why do you leave me
alone with this pen
the devil caught your heart
again, i see....

it's a cement summer
inside my soul
i pray for the tide
to come in
waiting until
i'm released from my sorrow
waiting 'til i can
find the dream-men

I GET A LOT OF ABUSE.
I TRY TO TAKE IT IN STRIDE.
WHEN YOU LEAVE YOUR GIRL
ALONE EVERY DAY
IT DOESN'T MAKE
FOR A REAL SMOOTH RIDE

IT DOESN'T MAKE GOOD SENSE
IN STRINGIN' ME ALONG
I STAY ALONE
AND NO MATTER WHAT
BABY, YOU'RE DOIN' ME WRONG

YOU CAN BE THE HOTTEST HERO
ON STAGE YOU CAN BE THE TOP SHELF
BUT YOU DON'T DELIVER
WHAT YOU SELL
IF 'YOUR CHICK' STAYS AT HOME
BY HERSELF

TALK ABOUT RINGS AND PERFUME
CARS THAT YOU PARK OUT BACK
I'M OUT HERE, A GIRL

IN THIS CRUEL, CRUEL WORLD
CARRYIN' MY LUNCH IN A SACK

HONEY, YOU'RE SO GOOD ABOUT IT
YOU BOOGIE LIKE YOU'RE ALMOST BLACK
BUT YOU'RE KILLIN' ME FAST
WHEN YOU LEAVE ME LAST
SPINNIN' MY WHEELS ON THE TRACK

I'M TRYIN' HARD TO GET IT TOGETHER
I'M GOIN' BACK TO SCHOOL FOR THE MAX
BUT THERE'S TOO MUCH STEAM
AND I GET REAL MEAN
AND I NEVER FIND A WAY TO RELAX

DON'T YOU EVER THINK ABOUT ME
THINK ABOUT WHAT'S REALLY MY SCENE
I AIN'T GOT A GUY
AND MY TANK'S ON DRY
YOU JUST DON'T COME DELIVER
MY DREAM

HONEY, YOU CAN SING ABOUT IT
I CAN SEE THAT YOU'RE RUNNIN'
FULL SPEED

BUT IT DON'T MEAN A THING
WHEN I'M CAUGHT IN BETWEEN
THE MUSIC AND THE MAN THAT I NEED

I DON'T MIND THE WORK OR THE EFFORT
I'VE GOT MY STUFF UNDER THE HOOD
BUT I AIN'T GOT A GUY
AND I THINK I'M GONNA DIE
DON'T BLAME ME IF IT
DON'T TURN OUT SO GOOD

I NEED YOU HERE BESIDE ME
I DON'T GIVE A SHIT
WHAT IT TAKES
GET YOURSELF HOME
'CAUSE I CAN'T STAY ALONE
AND THIS IS THE DEAL
I'M GONNA MAKE

I AIN'T GONNA WAIT FOREVER
YOU'RE NOT THE ONLY ONE
WHO'S SO HOT
I'M BURNIN' UP INSIDE
AND I JUST GOTTA RIDE

DON'T TELL ME YOU'RE SOMETHING
YOU'RE NOT

LIVIN' ON BARBS AND VIRTUE
TRYIN' TO KEEP MY TRIP COOLED OUT
BUT I CAN'T GET A START
AND IT TEARS ME APART
YOU KNOW WHAT THAT MUSIC'S
ALL ABOUT

IT AIN'T ABOUT MAKIN' HIT RECORDS
IT AIN'T ABOUT THE GIRLS
IN NEW YORK
THE KEY'S IN THE CAR
AND I'M WAITIN' AT THE BAR
AND I'M GIVIN' OUT FREE LESSONS
IN TORQUE

HONEY, YOU CAN SING ABOUT IT
YOU CAN BOOGIE, BABEE, 'TIL
YOU TURN BLACK
BUT I AIN'T GOT A MAN
AND I DON'T UNDERSTAND
WHAT I'M DOIN'

ON THIS RACECAR TRACK
IN MY PINK CADILLAC
CRUSHED VELVET SEATS
WAITIN' AT THE LIGHT
GIVIN' OFF THE HEAT

DICE HANGIN' DOWN
FOOT TO THE FLOOR
GIVIN' YOU A SIGN
RACE YOU ONE MORE
IN MY PINK CADILLAC
CRUSHED VELVET SEATS
PORTAWALL TIRES
AND SLICKS ON THE STREET

GET ROMANCE!

there's a lot of things
i do each day
and no one sees at all
i fix eggs and toast
and feed the cat
and locate my little girl's ball
i always stay alone
i must seem to fit the part
the life i lead is full of work
but there's romance in my heart

(CHORUS)
give me a night of romance
a little stardust in my eyes
give me more
than this cloudy day
it can make your river run dry
give me a slow dance, baby
i swear i just got a bad start

the job i do doesn't suit a girl
with so much romance in her heart

don't be so condescending
to a lady who appears uptight
sometimes there's things
        you don't realize
in private, she just might
be all right
she never said she did it easy
the faster the heartbeats...she runs
the soul is willing but the outside
...goes all undone

(CHORUS)
i lived a life of sorrow
these are things i can never say
i've been alone so long by now
even my feet...just turn away
but the spirit never wavers
i was a wild horse tryin' to pull a cart
running along the hillside thinkin' 'bout
all the romance inside of my heart

who could say, 'get romance'
to a girl who's been turned away
how can you get some magic goin'
when there's no one around
to play?
how can you win at horseshoes
and dance close, like you'll never
be apart
when you're all by yourself in the window
wishin' for the romance
that's stuck in your heart...

give me a night of romance
a little magic in my eyes
give me more
than another job
i'll wait till the river
runs dry
give me a slow dance, baby
i swear that was a bad, bad
        start
the life i lead
doesn't suit me none
'cause there's romance
in my heart

i know you wonder, baby
what's goin' on with me
you wonder if my love is gone
not how it used to be
well, don't you worry, darlin'
just set your mind at ease
look out across the ocean there
and feel a stir in the breeze

it's a pretty day with you, babe
there ain't another man in my heart
it's a day all right for havin' fun
as long as you share all the parts
this world can really take you down
if there's no one home for you
don't you worry about me, baby
or start wonderin' what we're gonna do

look back on the past, sweet baby
you know i've been right there
sometimes i'd yell and have a big tantrum
but always, you knew i cared
as time rolls on i'm like a mack truck

bustin' out on the street.
but that's just 'cause i love you, baby
the way you love me's so neat

i know you wonder
about me, baby
wonder about my good heart
and sometimes you even
doubt my good intentions
it's been a problem
right from the start
don't you dare
sit 'round thinkin'
'bout all these fools you see
this life is short
i plan on havin'
the life the lord promised to me

i know you wonder, baby
wonder about my style
you can buy it for
some green stamps, honey
i've been lovin' you all the while
every highway brings me back

to where i feel at home
you make my wheels keep turnin' 'round, babe
i never feel alone

i know you wonder, baby
what's goin' on with me
you wonder if my love is gone
not quite how it used to be
well, don't you worry, darlin',
i'll be your baby tonight (Rita Coolidge)
just reach over there
and flick that light off
everything will be all right...

she's a modern-day hero
worthy of respect
she sits
wounded in the window
dying of neglect
the dreams that dance around her
have frightened him away
she's a modern-day hero
here to save the day

oh, nothing is important
today is fading fast
and yesterday don't matter
do you dwell against the past
if those hours that i loved you
are really nothing in the end
then you really didn't love me
it was all a sin

i'm a modern-day hero
i sacrifice so well
and nothing really matters

without you
here is hell
tho i ramble like a gypsy
what this life has done to me
i'm your modern-day hero
where the hell is he

the future lurks among you
what will it be
will he take it all away from you
take a look at me
it was dreaming in the high style
it made me skip a beat
this is a modern-day story
the ending's not so neat

she's a modern-day hero
she stretches in the sun
the pace just made her reckless
watch her gazes run
she's a modern-day hero
champion of swords
listening to his heart-strings
listening to the chord
of the modern-day hero

worthy of respect
sitting in the window
dying of neglect

the horses are all in the stable
the cows are out under the moon
when are you coming home, baby
when will it be
i hope you come soon

it's been months, many days
since i've tarried
alone on this path of my tears
i looked quite up close in the mirrors
and saw that i've traveled
this pathway for years

wandering thru these dark hallways
praying for some sort of light
i looked 'neath the sheets
in my bedroom
and found it the middle of night

you of the white-throated dream song
sing all my sorrows away
hold me and tell me

you've loved me this long
hold me close, beg me to stay

the dream in my heart
never alters
nor packs up to leave me
in haste
the dreams of my love
for you, babe
have run thru my soul
laid my laughter to waste

how could you be such a cruel one
you, with your women and whims
waiting to bait you like the spiders
waiting
in the shadows
to hold you again

while i stand alone
at attention
my shoes have a shine
like this glass
and although you may find me

forsaken

this dream that i honor

shall help me stand fast

GET DRESSED UP

(CHORUS)
get dressed up
meet my baby tonite
get dressed up
you know i feel outta site
get dressed up
i got some lovin' to do
get dressed up, now baby
go meet you

get dressed up
you know i work all day
get dressed up
it's not often that i play
get dressed up
put my heart on the line
get dressed up
gonna have a funky time

get dressed up
you know i washed my car
get dressed up
so i'd look good at the bar
get dressed up
you've got me so turned on
gonna get dressed up
until it's all gone

get dressed up
you're a most important man
get dressed up
try to make you understand
get dressed up
and give you my best grin
get dressed up
and get ride those trims
and there we go again

father, you know i'm just a little guy
lookin' around down here
lotta dust in my eyes
and ya know, these folks
didn't hear what you said
about treatin' men as brothers
they hate each other instead

if i could have
just a little time
to work all day
making the bright lite shine
pull us all together
we're on a boat about to go...
if i could only reach out
and make the good things grow

they're killing each other off
like a man starved at sea
they're being real envious
that's no way to be
they don't seem to care
how they get their way

your folks are greedy monsters
who live to have their day

not one for silence
as i look around
see all the blood
on the streets and in the towns
i hear the ladies weeping
i hear the children cry
these people don't know how to live
they only want to die

in the sunny morning
you can see my father's house
it sits up on the hillside
like a bride who lost her spouse
if only men could realize
the folly of their deeds
we could make the earth a garden
fit to grow the seeds

watching out my window
the curtains blow with the breeze
i see the children playing
untouched by man's disease

i will give my life away

if only for a change

in the way that people come here, lord

why do they act so strange...

2002
Merry Christmas

some girls live for houses
get me a mansion on a hill
and give it everything they've got
to get the boy who will
some girls live for gold and jewels
they grab it when they can
but there's one thing
that keeps me here
i live for just one man

he's far away up north
where it's cold from dawn 'til dusk
he lives with people that he loves
his friends are who he trusts
he hardly even knows me
but i know his every thought
i live within the world he rules
and it's everything i've got

i live my life
for just one man
i've given up—
do what i can

if this is love
it's gonna kill me soon
there's no release
there's just no room

someday he'll come
and it will be
he'll look in my eyes
and find out it's me
he may never bother
he may never understand
how hard i live my life
for just one man

just one man
i'm waiting at his door
just one man
it could be so much more
i've waited for years
they say it can't be real
if this is just a fantasy
i've made it my big deal

just one man
gonna carry me home

just one man
oh, i stay so alone
just one man
in my window, staring there
just one man
and i've just got this prayer

baby, let me in
i've wanted you so long
hold out your hand to me
i can hardly carry on
these things in my mind
are driving me insane
i'd give all the time
that's left
just to meet again.

reach out to me
you can help me survive
i can do anything
if you'll just keep me alive
there's so much to live for
and i am fading fast
hold me thru the night, baby
make this nightmare pass

i live my life
for just one man
he's strong as the wind
and light as the sand
he moves like a wild colt
in the dark night on a hill
i'll live my life
for just one man
until i get my fill.

when i fall asleep at night
you're always on my mind
although you don't believe this truth
maybe i'll convince you
in time
you may think you've hands-on knowledge
you may think you've got me down
but the night you heard me calling out
i knew there was someone comin' 'round

i heard you at the front door
the chain was on the lock
you sounded just like horses
running around
my apartment lot
you were sitting by the tv
i thought you were someone else
if i had known it was you there, baby
i'd have come out and introduced myself

prowlers in the kitchen
grocery bags everywhere
how'd you like the kitty litter

the wallpaper needed repair
did you see the chairs i painted
i threw them out later on
like the t-shirt i had on those nights
i threw them out
after you had gone

remember about the witches
those things foretold to me
it was a homemade reel-to-reel, i heard
describing those things to be
it began with different noises
motorcycles (baby, i'm not deaf)
it ended with helicopters
(is that the way you left??)

you should know by now you're dealing
with the boys who run the show
and they ain't no ticket-takers
they're the boys who always glow
and me, i'm their bartender
i sweep up the floors at night
and sometimes i travel very far
and sometimes i ride the great light

the things i hold close to me
are those that have no words
the love that sits inside me
takes off to you like a bird
about my father's business
my home has streets of gold
and there i hoard no money
and there i never grow old

believe me when i tell you
i love you on my knees
you bring to me those things i hold

i remember

the time moving slowly

perched on a hilltop was i

caught by the wind

and the faceless tormentor

tripped

with the sand

stored up inside

he was there

as a shadow

in the future

always, he appeared

against the wall

stricken, silhouetted

he held the hourglass

i could see him come:

he was wild

and he was tall

he stood

as the shadow

in the hallway

many years
he took that place
and never ran
and once
he crossed back over
into my heartside
he let himself inside me
like a real man

but he's still there
against the backdrop
of all my hunger
so dark and silent, still
he scrapes the glass
i know
he is my husband
set out to greet me
but he's still lost
a shadow there
he binds me fast

and what becomes of us?
i love his shadow
it tells me all his stories
it can find

and i sit and listen there
within my heartside
waiting
for the man
he left behind

ah, it must be some
plot to deceive me
some sordid tale
to tame
my restless mind
i turn
and weave among
these thoughts that grieve me
and watch
this shadow dancing
that i find

i'm gonna live my life
serving the boss's world
when people see me on the street
they'll say, there goes
the bruce springsteen girl...

i'm proud to call him darlin'
and i hold him in my dreams
i give to him my loyalty
i'll show him what blue blood means

and as the years roll by,
it's okay, they can laugh at me if they will
it's no waste to love someone
if you just can't get your fill

i lost my heart to that boy
there ain't no turnin' back
lost my soul to rock-'n-roll
it's a real true heart attack
he may never be my husband
we may never have our son

but when the lord calls out my number
i'll know i raced and won

he's the only thing that matters
he's the spirit in my eyes
he's given me the life of a queen
and i ain't never gonna give him no lies
i know people have their problems
we're all strangers to this world
the one thing that really turns my wheels
is that i'm the bruce springsteen girl

Listen here, you bad-assed groupies
i'm the baddest of the whole bunch
i may never own the man i love
and i may never come back from lunch
but i love him like the gypsy
who dances to the merry men's band
i kick my heels real high to the beat
it's something most folks never understand

i'm the boss' baby
a distinction that makes me complete
whether or not i win his ring
i sing in the key of e-street

i've lived this life a soldier
i've gambled and i've lost
i'll live throughout the rest of my days
amazed at how little it cost

you know, it's such an honor
to be a bad ass in a bad land
i'll never get my fill of him
the boss and the boys in the band

mother, as a postscript
i'll become your model child
i'll work all day and eat your food
and never let myself run wild
i'll get a good job in my hometown
and live wherever you are
but my heart and soul and high-heel sneakers
are married to that rock-'n-roll star

boss, you know i love you
ain't no one in this world for me
i'll wait for you
like a horse out to pasture
a granny in sneakers and a tee
boss, you know i love you

it'll carry me thru this life

and when i die, i won't even cry

i'll be waitin' as

your rock-'n-roll wife.

if i could find somebody
who'd take my heart
i'd gladly go and give it away
but year in, year out
it never seems to work
and at this point
i'd even pay.

CHORUS

> who wants this heart of my own
> i'll sell it for cheap, now
> you can have it on loan
> i'd beg, steal, or borrow
> to get what i need
> a good man to love me
> a man who won't leave

you'd think by now
i'd have found me a man
who'd work with me all day
and play when i can
a man who is tender
with a heart just for me

you'd think by now
someone would have found the key

(CHORUS)
the baby has grown up
a girl who sees me grieve
a mom who is desperate
with tears all down her sleeve
a mom who's alone
each and every night
my little girl just holds me
and tells me, mom, it's all right

(CHORUS)
i sit in the window
the place where i dream
and i think of all the lovin'
that i've never seen
and i wonder if somewhere
he knows he's the one
and he'll open with the flowers
that come out in the sun

> who wants? this heart of my own
> i'll sell it for cheap, now

it's all that i own
i'm gonna beg, steal, or borrow
and get me what i need
a man who will love me
a man who'll never leave

laugh at me
shoot me a bird
leave me at the bus stop, baby
put out the word
say i'm a whore
make me a tramp
run me up and
down your ramp

i'm used to abuse:
the boy's name is bruce
and my neck's in a noose
we need to call a truce
i'm used to abuse
used to abuse

masquerade
it's your game
as usual
i get the blame
stick out your tongue
boo and hiss

up yours, baby
that's your kiss

i'm used to abuse
and i'm just hangin' loose
with my neck in a noose
used to abuse

i get high
and you're down there
it's much better
i need some air
you're so weird
you're the boss
the stakes are always
at my cost

i'm used to abuse
the dude's name is bruce
and we need to call a truce
used to abuse
i'm used to abuse
used now to bruce
used to abuse

i wish we could lay down
by the fire tonight
and melt away with the sun
        a walk in the park
        as it grows dark
knowing
our battle was won

i wish we could be
together just once
and turn back the hands
that have failed
        to join us as one
        a'glow in the sun
i'd take to the sea
with my sails

i wish i could be
happy inside
with you, there, alone
by the fire
        but the dream fades away
        another ordinary day
i'm alone here, again
up for hire

i wish we could be
two people so close
running away
in the fire
        running somewhere
        all the people care
but it's a bad act
and i fell off
the high wire

i wish we could be
just what i dream
in a house, with the kids
by the fire
        but you'd want to get out
        you don't know what
        i'm about
somewhere
in this dream
you're a liar.

i wish we could be
i just wish he would see
the cookies in the oven
near the fire

    i love these old dreams
    tho they're not
    what they seem
and they've gone and
turned me into
some fool buyer...

i can take whatever
they can dish out
i got my flag unfurled
if you'll only
play with me, baby
'cause i'm just
your basic girl

my hand's in my pocket
i can whistle a tune
or kiss your toes
till they curl
if you'll only
come 'round to see me
honey, i'm just
your basic girl

basic girl
basic girl
we're all livin' in a basic world
basic girl
basic girl

i know i'm livin'
in a real weird world

walk with me, baby
uptown tonight
you get me
in such a swirl
you're so cute
i freak right out
but still i'm
your basic girl

basic girl
basic girl
we're all livin'
in a real slick world
basic girl
basic girl
i know i'm alive in
a real sick world

he seems to know
what i need
he caught the heart
that i hurled

so maybe he's gonna
hold me tonight
hold on to
his basic girl

basic girl
basic girl
we're all livin'
in a basic world

please, baby,
give it one more chance
how could you deny me
my pleasure
you forget about me
and take what you need
but baby, it's
measure for measure...

measure for measure
give me my half
you take what you want
you leave me and laugh
what are you thinking
you are so mean
you're the most heartless
man and i'll see you come clean

do you know how I'm feeling
each day so alone
the tears on my pillow
the pain in me has grown
and everywhere i turn

you cut like a knife
the spider is caught
taking her own life

i can't go on
these things that haunt me
i can't stay alone
isn't someone there for me?

i poured the cup
so i'll drink the wine
you'll never have the secrets
locked up in my mind
but what do you care
it's just your game
your money for admission
everyone
protects your name

i've lost in the end
what i wanted is gone
lost in the notes
i used to sing along
and the only contentment
i might find for relief

is someone 'neath the streetlights
who'll come home and share my grief

why couldn't you step out
and say hello to me
are you that big a STAR
your neon blinded me
but your glow unplugs
when the electricity ebbs
you're the mean plastic man
who tore up her web

measure for measure
look at what you did
i'm a wreck on the highway
I'm no mom for a little kid
i want you to know
that my time has run out
steamrollered by the boy
i used to dream about

measure for measure
and my own backward glance
makes me sick

in the mirrors
and i never got a chance

please, baby,
give it one more try
how could you deny me
leave me to cry
you forget about me
and take for your pleasure
but baby, it's
measure for measure

call me up, honey
i'm at home tonite
it's been a long time waitin' for ya
i want to do ya right

my fingers are crossed
my rabbit's foot's on
when are you comin' 'round here
hope you won't take long

> promises, promises
> his promises are sweet
> give me a bunch of promises
> to make my night complete

> promise me everything
> and give me your all
> your promises, baby
> make me stand up tall

take me to dinner
pizza or chinese

look in my eyes, baby
show me your tease

i'm wild about you
i just love you all
i love all your promises, baby
why won't you call

    promises, promises
    his promises so sweet
    sugar on my honeycomb
    he's my special treat

    promise me anything
    but give me your stuff
    your promises, baby
    and i'm full of the fluff

you stay so busy
(but they told me you'd come...)
out here to make it right
you know you're the one

nothing's good without you
my life is a waste

without your promises, baby
i'll need another face

promises, promises
boy of my heart
sneakin' 'round my bedroom
givin' me a start

why try to steal
what's yours there to take
promises with sugar, babee
give me a break.

she lives in her ivory tower
lost to the sounds of his touch
tosses and turning all night
will he come back:
        she wants him so much

she stares out the chipped-away window
half-eaten strings lace the floor
maybe he'll be here tomorrow
but he never
        comes back to her door

she's been there
alone by the fire
for years, as the sand slips away
sometimes the sunlight falls on her glance
you can tell nothing matters
        this way
but the lines that she draws
of his features
she knows them so well from inside

she touches no one
    in the mirrors
alone, there's just no place to hide

obsessed with the love of a hunter
possessed by the whiff of his song
she sits in her ivory tower
dying
    the waiting is long

the stones in the walls of her chamber
as grey and as cold as her mind
she repeats his name to the fire
the sand slips away with the time

all the day suffers the longing
and in the night escapes relief
darkness hovers like pigeons
with poems and rubber bands on their feet

    you of the clouds and my murmurings
    you of the knight's punctured tune
    you of my breath and my horror
    you, painted man on the moon...

i don't have much
you know i'm poor
but all i had
was yours, for sure
when i thought of you
my soul was warm
a place for comfort
shelter from the storm

now you've torn
that world apart
you killed the love
inside of my heart

came in the night
a thief with black gloves
paid off someone
and gave me a shove
stole what i had
then you walked away
you're bad off, baby
i'll see you pay

you left me alone
you tore me apart
you've gone and killed the love
inside of my heart

you take from those
who've nothing for their own
you who have everything
the criminal on his throne
pretty hungry women
to feed your glutton face
you broke the Law, baby
now live with your disgrace

made me feel so cheap
right from the start
you've killed the love
inside my heart

i begged you to hold me
give me relief
turn around the insults
help me find some peace
you coward with your money

your fame, position—keep.
the horror of the moment
runs in me this deep

borne in me a dead man
who's torn my world apart
you killed the love
inside my heart.

he's my baby
he's also my guy
i love him so much
each day i just die
he holds me and whispers
it'll all work out in time
and he loves me in the darkness
he's my partner in crime

partners in crime
a pact with our souls
runners on fire
so hot that we're bold
in the tolling of the vessel
we signed the bottom line
now, forever after
we are partners in crime

i can't live without him
but he lives without me
evading all the chances
still, it had to be
foretold of this story

and of these ties that bind
now, unveil the masquerade
partners in crime

partners in crime
he's done it to me
it was love on the line
now he set us free
haunted by visions
i grasp these hands of mine
give me something to hold on to
sweet partner in crime

looking back on it
it hurts a little there
the bruises on my lips
the marks on my stare
i wish he had shown me
his secrets that are mine
we were victims of the witches
become partners in crime

partners in crime
(it was) foretold to me
captured from behind

oh, he set us free

victims in the story

i've no shame that's mine

i love the man who touches me

my partner in crime

now hold on there, honey
you done got it all wrong
the roof on my house fell in
and done broke all o'yo songs

now in my room it's rainin'
and there's creepy things movin' in
but you know i ain't complainin'
i'm just lettin' you know
the roof done fell in

i swear, we get so messed up
i don't know how we survive
we got some wild imagination
and i suppose it keeps us alive

but now here's my situation
you done broke my heart in half
and i sit here, huddled in my bedroom
listenin' to all you hot shots laugh

while the creepy things are movin' in
and i'm movin' out—that's right

i can't stay here for the burglars
so i gotta move my stuff outta site

and honey, this brings up another point
you know i ain't got no home
but listen here, i ain't complainin'
sometimes i just feel sorta alone

and what's that stuff about the last time
the only last time i know
was that weird dude down at the bus stop
who missed out 'cause he was too slow

and one more thing now, baby
since i got your ear—let's talk.
what's that stuff about what i got
from here, baby, it ain't a whole lot

it ain't the hard times that got me
and i ain't complainin'—tell steve.
it's the night after night anticipatin'
and the night after night that it leaves

now you know we all need somebody
i tried a million times to do it right

but you made a puppet of my heartstrings, baby
you pushed me out with the monsters in the night

and who's that girl who ain't so pretty
whose lovin' arms are all you need?
when you see her tell her she's lucky
to still have her two front teeth

i know you think i'm touché
i know you imagine what you can
honey, i'm a woman who gets lonely
don't make me miserable
to be what i am

and last of all, boss, remember,
this ain't no jive honky girl
you ain't found yourself some turkey, baby
you done found yourself the best chicken
in the world.

southern fried

hey, do ya want me
to sit up all nite and cry
with a lump in my throat
and these tears in my eyes

i can't believe
you still might care
after all this time
why don't we turn and
go out there...

there, where the wind is soft
there, we can take a walk
there, the summer never ends
there, where i go when i
need a friend

is it possible
or is it something i make up
that a guy like you
could make me
strut my stuff

and act real bad
even tho i'm shy
make me feel so good
as the world goes by

there must be a key
to open up your door
the damn thing's stuck
i'll put my bags down
on the floor
and kick it in
        ain't nothin' ever
        kept me back
is it really true
or is there
        something else i lack

i know you're home
you gave those girls a ride
and my car won't start
don't ya want me
        at your side
or maybe
there's someone i don't know

who's there tonite
stealin' my show

why won't you come
unlock this door
the damn thing's stuck
and my heart's so sore
maybe i'll wait
right out there
for you, baby
if you really care...

you didn’t want me
when i was a saint
no man in my bedroom
no one to taint
and you didn’t want me
when i was a whore
no one beside me
just john at my door

you didn’t want me
and i’ve had my fill
you don’t want me, baby
and it makes me stand still
when someone you love
just lets you walk away
i got the message, baby
i hear what you say

i know i’m not much
but i’m told the right man
could have made me feel good
satisfied with what i am
you could’ve made me

stand up and feel great
but you chose to laugh
and i went home to escape

who knows what
you are...not me.
but i know you're not
the boy you used to be.
i said it once
and i'll say it again
i'm still the same
with whom or within

these windows i make
have spots from the rain
my tears trickled down
that's what's left of the pain
an eager window-washer
    it's my job
to pile up the sadness
into one big glob
and throw it in the trash
like you did with me
used me to your advantage
make your money for free

songs for free—
remember that one?
i thought it was silly
but now it's no fun
ain't nothin' free
but this mess on the floor
the red mask on your face
baby, you evened up the score

a mirror for her
the teaser in this play
tormented from the angles
and the things he used to say
So weary from the years
of a game that came undone
little girl lying
in the mud
        not the sun.

have a heartbreak, baby
'cause that's all i've got
and lots of time to think about
all the things i'm not
leave with your friends
—you're never alone

but i'll see you one day

after we've gone back home...

a thirty-day notice, babe
that's what you get
no more plastic romance
my mind has been set

pack your belongings
turn in your key
a thirty-day notice
gonna vacate me

thirty-day notice
thirty-day leave
we placed at romance
don't wanna grieve
thirty days until
i'm bound to be free
can't take all this bullshit
turn in your key

i'll wash the sheets
i'll dust the room
rid of that man
who smothers my tune

out in the streets
i'll send him away
he got a thirty-day notice
i ain't gonna pay

i love you so much
and i felt like such a fool
i should have known
you've been to that school
i should have seen
you watching over there
i should have known—
baby, why won't you
        show me you care

show me you care
take me thru the long night
hold out your hand
someone blew out my light
show me you care
can't you see i'm at the end
how strong can i get
you know it's all pretend

i need you so much
i was crushed at the scene
nervous and drugged
blew my head from another dream

if i could close my eyes
and make it go away
baby, show me you care
i'm gonna die and fade away

show me you care
hold my hand thru the night
show me you care
half the rent'll be all right
it's a sin the way you are
when i need you here with me
no other guy
does what you do to me

i can try to forget
and i can play a little game
but it turns the glass darkly
as i call out your name
and i wonder in the twilight
who sees, when i'm alone
but now i know you're out there
baby, why won't you
    give me a ride home.

and show me you care
touch me 'til i can't speak
numb from the salt
and the things you repeat
show me you care
half as much as me
i'd do anything
if you'd come home to me.

show me you care
i sent him away
he was just a kid
and we were gonna play
show me you care
is it so much to you
can't you give a little bit
baby, you know i'm
          just a fool.

show me you care
honey, look the other way
turn your back on me
a fool caught in her play
do you show me you care
when you hold her all night

we know it works both ways
to make it all right

show me you care
you—you never turn real
you're just bunches of words
not a very good deal
you never show me you care
'cause you're never around
you just stick with the
          albatross
as the music turns the clown.

show me you care
this nightmare is too long
you own my heart
and you own my song
what more do you want
from me,
i'm just a fan
who fell in the dark night
lookin' 'round for her man...

got some news for you now
i am sedated
went to a doctor
who was so educated
one look at me
he knew i'z under stress
the pain in my face
had made me a mess

i'm tellin' you
that i got sedated
don't give a damn
which way i get rated
oh, i can do it
it don't bother me
i'm feelin' so good
yeah, it's the life for me

hey there, honey
well, i got sedated
and it's all right
that my shiny halo's tainted

left my hometown happy
filled with little pills
made me feel much better
took away my ills

oh, so good
and you won't hurt me now
i am sedated
got loose anyhow
oh, the corner drugstore
has really got the stuff
you're never alone
you can always get enough

i'm so glad now
nothin' bothers me
i am sedated
smashed as i can be
see you in my bedroom
your plastic record screams
but it's okay
i'm sedated in my dreams...

i've waited for you, babe
the years have come and gone
i kick around the pebbles
i hum all your songs
and i do the dishes
and i watch tv
i knew one day i'd run into
the boy made just for me

rainy day, darlin'
you're my rainy-day friend
let the world pass by
this day never end
hold me and tell me
it's gonna be all right
i got a rainy-day sweetheart
thru the long, lonely nights

what took you so long, boss
i think you got scared
thought i was a wizard
who flew around in the air

but i'm just a poor girl
who could never let it out
i only tell my secrets
to the boy i dream about

he's my rainy-day darlin'
my rainy-day friend
he lets the world go by
and he makes my worries end
he holds me and he whispers
it's gonna be all right
got me a rainy-day sweetheart
to turn around my nights

now it's a blue day
a grey day again
wishin' he was with me
to help me pretend
in my imagination
he holds me this way
he's my rainy-day darlin'
but he's always far away

rainy-day darlin'
my hopes never end

wonder if he'll come into
my window again
someday he'll hold me
and it's gonna be all right
i keep lovin' my sweetheart
thru these long rainy nights

i could never satisfy you, baby
you need a woman
made of other stuff
someone who can
cater to your wishes
someone who will
want you when you're ruff

i could never give you
what you're wanting
i can hardly hold myself
upright
driven in the darkness
by the memories
half-suspended
i hear your voice all night

it's something new to me
a man who whispers
and tells me things
i've never known alone
teasing me and driving me
asunder

the little want in me
has become grown

i know you'll swear
you'd never hurt me, baby
the way of love
sits still until we call
and then it overtakes
the strongest soldiers
and binds us to someone
to stand or fall

a temper full of passion
and you'd kill me
it doesn't take so much
to smell revenge
one day as my lover
and another
enemies
you'd get me in the end

and tho you think me
just a bitch to harness
i'm not always
the weak one that i seem

iron hands aroused
within my pockets
in my heart
the vision of my dreams

i told you once
about the ghost within me
and i am bound
to give him what he asks
whenever it is time
to do my duty
i go to him
and finish up my tasks

of this world
i walk in purple flowers
robes and jewels and sonnets
in my eyes
and tho i may seem to be
another lady
the things you see
are just a good disguise

i could give you handcuffs
for your whimsies

or cords and ropes and shackles
—make you high
but sometimes this tenderness
within me
makes me want
to let those things
go by...

the tormented teaser
with her hair bleached out
she moans to the music
a sneer around her snout
she knows it's all over
as her number is called
but she really doesn't care much
her trip is gettin' balled

tormented teaser
in the shadows she stands
hungry and hidden
looking for her man
she knows he's out there
with a dream in his heart
but she just can't seem to find him
and it tears her apart

she's the tormented teaser
someone's wife in the store
spending her time
on the nickel-and-dime floor
and she's hot for adventure

you'd never suspect
and she whispers and she murmurs
always holding half a deck

the tormented teaser
a fool who's turned too old
writhing and thrashing
as her story gets told
and no one can save her
from the road she rambles on
her highway is empty
and her toys are all gone

she's just a teaser
bored to the core
begging and pleading
as each man gives her more
but she never stays
and they never ask why
the tormented teaser
with nothing to buy

she's the girl in the mirror
she's this pain on my face
giving me away as i

make such a sad case
and i know it was good
but i break up in flight
from the tormenting echoes
that torture me all night...

call the cards

call the cards

oh, my heart's

got it so hard

call the cards

call the cards

i'm so hot

and it's so hard

this is it

i've had enuff

i sit and watch

you strut your stuff

and i can't move

no, i can't speak

i think of you

my soul is weak

there's none i need

i live alone

but there is one

i'd carry home

he's just a boy
i'd be his girl
but he is gone
the dream i twirl

i can't wait
i can't hold on
he's got to come
and take me home

this is it
the last chance, babe
i call the cards
the dues are paid

call the cards
call the cards
i'm so hot
and it's so hard

call the cards
call the cards
i've had enough
i've got the hards

he was holdin' me in his arms
tellin' me he's gonna make me his own
and he put some more money by my bed
as he left me in my room alone
and i kept repeating your name
to myself, chase the tears away
it was you there, honey, holdin' me close
tellin' me it's okay

the life i lead gets to me
ain't no runnin' 'way from this pain
for two cents, babe, i'd call you up
and ask you what the hell is your game

he calls at 3 a.m.
he wants to come over, please
and then he lays out
those hundred-dollar bills
and leaves me there at home on my knees
no, you don't know about this
and honey, what would you do anyway
you're out there being number one
while i'm here with nothin' left to say

the life i lead gets to me
it's your lovin' on my mind
for two cents, babe, i'd call you up
and beg for a little of your time

i'll survive the insults
and i'll make it thru another day
there's no chance to turn him down
'cause i've got the rent to pay
you in your world can't imagine
how the time binds me so tight
and squeezes out what i hold inside
and never seems to make it all right

the life i lead gets to me
i'm a fool caught in this play
for two cents, babe, i'd call you up
but there'd be nothin' i could say

i've always been
kinda satisfied
with livin' my life
on a fast freeride
i never wondered
what speed to keep
i keep her to the floor
and listen for the heat

i always wanted
to see what's goin'
on with everybody else
everywhere i've gone
i figured it'd keep
my feet on the ground
one foot to the floor
the other one
tappin' out the sounds

i never knew
it might turn out this way
part of me lost and
the other part

waitin' for the day
and now they tell me
i'll spend my life alone
next time—to pay for
these sins i've sown

well, hell, bring it on
you know i'll pay the price
for watchin' what was happenin'
when they let go of the dice
i'd say the dude's worth it
but they say he'll let me down
i'm gonna try it, hey
no more of these sad, lonesome towns

gonna let him know
i'll be his girl
sixty years old
still in ribbons and curls
this is who i need
to help me get it right
the dude's got it straight
gonna prove it all night

so step on it, buddy
got a lot to do
this life without you
ain't nothin' but blue
i'll hold on
but just a little longer
i got a wild hair
i ain't gettin' any stronger

foot to the floor
and i'm ready at the wheel
gonna pass you this joint
and see if we got a deal
my ass in gear
and i'm headin' for the line
this sweet baby's
gonna be all mine...

i find an anonymous mailbox
hoping the postman won't know
it's me
writing to you, boss
this whole thing
is gonna lay me
a big blow

i look around
for witnesses
and slide it into
the slot
and then i go back
to my regular things
foolish and restless and hot

i succumb to the fate
of the loneliest girls
i wrote to a star
far away
and now people talk
i see their mouths move
but i hear

nothing
they say

i fell in love
with my stereo
i know it sounds weird
but it's true
where to begin
if he sings even when
the record
has played the song thru...

curled up in my bed
puffing on my pipe
reading words about
how to live my life

still we're not together;
i wonder what we've done
wanted you so much
the windows have been sprung

everything's invaded
disheveled in this room
where your soul has cried to mine
i live within this tomb

who am i but
some familiar bloke
who's turned away
wishing for a stolen rush
as i gamble all of these days

a soldier
a maid

a mother
a whore
all of these names
and still i need more

i want to see
the sweat on your face
from hours of breathing
with me in this place

big drops of moonlight
slide down your skin
they make me wipe you
again and again

hours to hold you
when the darkness has grown
among those things that
i claim for my own

it's my religion
expression of fact
the sun in my womb
and the soft dream attack

hold my gaze long
when we lie close thru the night
for i hide the prisoner
who gives me the light...

i miss you so much
as i sit here in my room
the music is movin'
and my head is in full bloom

what do you think about
what does it seem
what do you remember
as they turn to you and scream

i've never had a friend
who had all of me
i'd like someone to be with
i wonder what we'd see

everything's much better
the tempo and the beat
everybody's actin' like
those things i had to eat

got a bad-assed attitude
and this is where i turn
and pop her up in third gear
and watch that baby burn

i never smiled
i never spoke
i was so freaked out
my knees was weak
i got a kid
and i'm always broke
and i never pass up
a long free toke

my life is lonely
my life is tough
i'm a working girl
and i never get enough
a home and a family
that's what i got
ain't nothin' fancy
and the rent sure cost a lot

hey dude, i wanna play your game
i pawned all my gold
and i need a new name

we live like orphans
we need a dad
we got a new kitty
and sometimes we're all sad

we like music
we like to have fun
but we work all the time
and there's never anyone
try to be cool
keep it in line
but sometimes the distance
just gets into my mind

i'm lookin' for ya, boss
everywhere i go
he's got your sideburns
this one's got your nose
a mom and a dad
the best i can be
takes a lot more help
than just me

hey dude, i wanna play your game
got a headful of daydreams
that got left out in the rain

doin' it alone
in this mixed-up world
makes a hardcore life
for a working girl....

love by proxy
that's what it's been
out all night
with another man again

it's been such a drag
these past few years
makes me wanna bust out
and pop her up in gear

love by proxy
it's a habit that i hate
wish i could change things
before it's too late

i know this guy
well, i've heard about this dude
he's got it on his shoulders
and all his friends are rude

but sometimes something happens
and it pulls him up tight

little thoughts creep into his
sometimes late at night

he knows i think about him
he knows i want to know
why it's love by proxy
such a bad, bad way to go

come on now, baby
you know you've got the stuff
it could be so easy, hey
you know i've had enough

of this love by proxy
i got to have the king
anything less is
not the real thing

love by proxy
been holdin' out for you
come on, baby, do it
you can make my dreams come true

love by proxy
makes me wicked and so ruff

give me what i need, i want
the best of the good, good stuff

love by proxy
he's a hard, cruel man
gonna take it to my grave
and i don't give a damn

it's been so long already
with the loneliness, the fear
and they sit tight on my shoulders
baby, don't make me wait another year

he'll come around again
in another year or two
he'll come to see his friends
and maybe he'll see you

he'll fly into the city
the boss is back in town
you can save yourself to meet him
or you can tear those dreams right down

don't you know a million girls
would love to catch his eye
or kiss him when he passes
or give his band a try

hey, you know i need you
what more can i say or do

i've done what i can from this side, baby
the rest is up to you

don't be that hard on me
i'm make of bricks and clay
and i only cry when left behind
honey, i cry every day

i know the good lord loves me
but i hate myself as i run
i tried to do the proper thing
and i missed out on the big one

a warm home and a family
little kids out in the sun
will it disappear before my eyes
before the bet's been won

i go to work each morning
i do the best i can
and i get down on my knees at night
and i pray for my one good man

i know i love you, baby
i belong to the stereo songs

that tell about my love for you
but they just spin around for so long.

will ya eject the diamond needle
it got stuck inside my heart
it tore a hole too big to fix
and it's tearing me apart

goin' on the third year
i've pleaded to you to come on
won't you be still and hold me, baby
i belong to the stereo songs...

we're victims of the moon and stars
poised to catch a glimpse
one the other, fairy-like
in a sweet romance that makes no sense

i was so ready for you, babe
that night on halloween
and i know that you were ready too
that night i failed to make the scene

we're victims of the moon and stars
i think of you all the time
there's never a moment without you, babe
you're always on my mind

i still wait alone here to hold you
will you come to see me real soon
the devil asleep in my window again
left me victim of the stars and the moon

come to me, honey, i need you
no one can stand in your place

you are the man of my laces and satins
the man who could step up the pace

we're victims of the moon and stars
turning our dreams to the light
rapid rehearsals casting our nets
waiting to catch the big bite...

how do you know
when he's on the stage
if you're the one
or if it's your age
who can you ask
when your heart's gone down
for the hottest dude
in tinsel town
if there's a chance
will you meet him somehow
will he call you at home
will he ever come 'round
and if you told your friends
they'd look at you strange
and think that the pressure
has narrowed your range

if you write to the man
you're just one more girl
he's hot to excite
as he tours the world
if you wait all night

just to get him alone
fact is, the boy will
ignore your sweet moans
so how do you know
when you heart's been caught
if he cares at all
what games you've been taught
he's the spotlight savior
and i'm under his spell
no word from the boss
but you never can tell

gonna go to my job
gonna wish on that star
to come here and save me
before i owe for a car
no other man
turns me on this a'way
for one piece of his ass
i'd sure give it away
if you can hear me, honey
you know i'm the one
who waits for a chance
to give you a son
if you're in red bank

miami - la

remember me, baby

i'm only a phone call away

there ain't no ties
that bind my heart
as i put her in gear
and feel the engine start
ain't no dude
make me walk the line
one voice i hear
and honey, that's mine.

i got some headstrong
highway headgear
and i move
along crowded avenues
i dig
the beat that i hear on the radio
wearin' out
my southern woman's shoes

a man can only
do so much
he thinks you're lucky
to have his touch

but he don't know
how much i got
it's a whole lot more
and i keep it real hot

don't implicate me
it's all your game
you won't get a chance
to make me the same
a life of freedom
won't get me down
'cause i'm wild and i'm bad
and i'm out on the town

he'll say i'm old
it'll burn me out
but i'll prove he's wrong
without a doubt
dreams and rainbows
fill up my tank
i'll run with the wind
and just me to thank

he's coming to atlanta
the boss is back in town
i heard it on the fm
the folks are gonna get down

i wonder if he'll call me
that's what my dreams imply
i wonder if he'll remember me
or if he'll pass my by

now, i'm not one for fussin'
i gave that boy his chance
he left me emptyhanded
without a backward glance

but that was in LA
and we know how angels fall
i wonder if he'll fix it up
or if he's born to stall

the boss is mighty headstrong
he wants to have his say

well, this is my home territory
We'll see who gets his way

i ain't gonna buy a ticket
he can do his show alone
as far as this one girl's concerned
he can do his thing and go home.

i thought about sending you poems
reluctant and eager—i sway
i know that you've found a sweetheart
and my, how she gets in the way

i'm happy you now have a person
no one should stand out alone
i just hope you tender your treasure
and love her and make her your own

and me, i fade into the backdrop
another day working for me
and i wonder why god holds the carrot
too high in my push to be free

i know that i'm given the best stuff
i've always held rainbows and charms
and maybe one day in this story
i'll fall into the right prince's arms

and as you go knowing my message
i hope you'll give life till the end

for the world and her children go hungry
weary from all of the men

and one day an old man,
you'll pass me tho i won't be a girl anymore
and maybe by then you'll have time, sir
to sit down and even the score

you were staring from the cover
of a well-known magazine
you were skating on the ice
and your face was lookin' mean
i clutched another song
and i was mailing it to you
but i opened up those pages
and you were holding someone new

i glanced at all the photographs
you had the secret of the world
you said it was in everything
but especially in that girl
my hands began to shake and sweat
as i tore apart your song
and i went home to my little girl
the ending was all wrong

i laid in bed that night distraught
i spent the year for nil
i couldn't bring the dream to life
against the windowsill
and i wondered how i fell so hard

for a man i never met
how could i let myself belong
to a dream i must forget

oh, god, please come release me
from his words, his voice, his tune
send me someone, anyone
make me forget him soon
my journey with the horsemen
flashing headless on these walls
and i crumble in the darkness
just a little girl, after all

it's been a heartfelt moment
that year i spent with you
now claiming all your secrets
and wondering if you felt it too
you can have your jets and actresses
you can have your touch of class
you can have success and bright lights, baby
it's just the window-glass

i was no one to you
i was just another fan
you would drive all night

for that girl's arms
that's how the story ran
and i remembered when i heard you
screaming from your heart and soul
and my tears mixed with the rain and slush
as i stepped into the cold

i find myself at home again
with no place left to turn
trading all the love i had
for another night to burn
i lean against the streetlamp
and i murmur to the men
who call me in the dark night
        now
'cause I'll hold them once
        again...

the tormented teaser
with his hair slicked back
he hums to the music
all his eggs in one sack
he knows he's got something
they like him this way
but he knows it's not real
just a game they all play

tormented teaser
light up this night
turn me around
and make it all right
push back the years
in the glass where i give
hand me some lovin'
and a reason to live

tormented teaser
he's a hero at best
and a boy running scared
with a heart that don't rest
and a fire that drives him

to the edge of the grave
—i know what he wants
and that's what i save

he's a tormented teaser
who's lonely inside
in the spotlight he calls me
but he won't give me a ride
and he tries from his soul
to right what is wrong
but he knows it's no good
and it's so hard to move on

the tormented teaser
a mirror for him
to see that he's only
a man—in the end
who carries his sorrow
it's wild in his eyes
and no one can comfort
his heart full of lies

he's just a teaser
tormented in pain
a little boy holding

all his toys in the rain
with mud on his trousers
and tears on his face
and he looks a bit rumpled
as he moves up in the race

he's the boy of my daydreams
he left me with this
another night empty
still wanting his kiss
and i know about him
we both have our ways
you can hear him on the radio
as the tormenting plays

put on my headphones
a two-record set from my man
ready to hear the new album
and all of a'sudden i understand
i followed the message
machine-gunned in my gut
listening to your sweet soul-cryin' boss
it makes me wanna grab your butt

> honey, come on
> i wanna kiss your ass
> you can delegate the future
> and i won't give you no sass

> baby, you got me
> with wings moving on my feet
> true love ain't no easy thing
> but it's sure got all the rest beat

now every nite i tune in
to you singin' in my ears
all alone in the living room
i'm with you loud and clear

the music's bustin' out
with everything i need
i can't believe you made those songs
and you're a'drivin' me on at this speed

baby, come on
i wanna kiss your ass
i love you and i ain't held you yet
and i'm headin' for ya wild and fast

there ain't no two ways about it
i wanna kiss your ass
this is what i've been waiting for
and i know it's gonna last

you got it, baby
you got it all over your face
there ain't another dude on this earth
that could ever take your place
there ain't no one
for me—but you—this way
babee, i got my hands on your jeans
and there's nothing else left to say

hey, come on
i wanna kiss your ass
you can have me for a dollar
and i ain't gonna give you no sass

boss, i dig you
it's gonna be a real gas
the rest is just a formality
you know i wanna kiss your ass

there i was

rent money in hand

runaway wife

hound for the promised land

my kid was at kathy's

my bags were all packed

i was at the airport

and i was never comin' back

> but oh, he didn't want me
>
> he didn't understand
>
> i didn't even see him
>
> i was just another fan
>
> just another lady
>
> with smooth and open legs
>
> just another hungry heart
>
> crawlin' as she begs

a ride to pasadena

an airport bus at 5 a.m.

it was there at the hilton

that i threw away his pin

he ain't nothin' to me
it'll never be repaired
i'm not so anxious anymore
just wounded where i cared

oh, he didn't want me
those songs were for the cash
he didn't wanna hold me
he just threw me in the trash

he said he'd hang my memory
in a box as his ideal
you know, the dude's just ignorant
of how this woman feels

i should have known better
than to go wasting my time
on a yankee from new jersey
with propriety on his mind

i thought that rock-'n-roll fellas
liked to play the game
i guess that when there's money involved
...everyone's the same

oh, he didn't want me
this witch just bit the dust
i was just another fan at 3 a.m.
tryin' to peddle her lust

oh, it was awful
i never thought i'd get so low
as to wait all night in the darkness
for the star of a rock-'-n-roll show

i was a fool
and that is a fact
i got to the LA airport
and i never looked back

now i owe my rent
and i had to unpack
and i lost a night's sleep
with my pride on my back

oh, he didn't want me
i was just another fool
willing with a hungry heart
ready to break the rules

oh, he didn't need me
all his friends were there
i was just some nasty incident
and he didn't even care

well, go to hell
you rock-'n-roll boy
go to bed
and keep all a'your toys

I've got my business
a child to 'tend
i don't have time
for chasin' after men

oh, he didn't want me
i almost fell in love
but everything got broken
in a sordid twisted shove

he showed me who was boss
and i hate him for it all
i guess i learn the hard way
how little angels fall...

at five o'clock this morning
i put your new tape on
and got under the headphones
and heard you sing my song

now i'm in the city
at my desk for the day
and i can still hear you, boss
lovin' these blues away

it keeps me at the crossroads
somehow you've given me life
inside my soul it's screaming out
to take away this knife

i'll be there mumbling something
i'll find out what i got
what's in it for me when the winds change
if i'm blowin' cold or hot

it's you, boss, ain't you somethin'
i'll never be the same

without your light in this darkness
hey—i'd have to change my name

give it to me, baby
i know it'll make me a man
movin' along those velvet rims
it's how i understand...

you say you'll be touring october
a two-record set from The Boss
bombarded again in my fantasies
oh, lord, how much
is this one gonna cost

distracted
in every situation
their eyes keep reflecting
your voice
why
are you driving me crazy
i guess i'm gonna listen
'cause there ain't no choice

i try to behave
and the mirror
laughs at me, teases
my glance
he was only a dude
in the spotlight
he was only my lover
hey, look at him dance

i've lost control
of my good mind
but i've got all the rest
by the balls
so is this the end of
the story or does it begin
as he
tears down the walls

at this point, i'll give it
the last ride
gonna put it in gear
let her out
how far you wanna bet
that she'll take me
to the edge of the darkness
where it makes me shout

success
and he goes to australia
i wonder
if he'll smoke in japan
i hope he remembers
        my good side
i hope that he knows
        he's my man

i wanna thank you, darlin'
for what you mean to me
i wanna turn around and hold you
as close as two people can be

i wanna take you all the places
i've traveled in my dreams
i wanna be a part of your life
i wanna be on your scene

i wanna take this opportunity
to tell you how i feel
i think you're a fine survivor
with both hands on the wheel

i never knew another man
more exciting in my eyes
to me there's not a single cloud
cluttering your friendly skies

oh, baby, when you sing
it makes my wheels go 'round

but more important, baby
is this love that i have found

religious, it's revival
you get me to my feet
standing up for everything
in this world we wanna keep

you made yourself a model
for your audience, your crowd
when you take us to the heartland
yeah, you make it nasty and loud

oh, i thank you, baby
for the gift you gave us all
a reason to be a better man
a reason not to fall

once upon a time
i went to a rock-'n-roll show
i learned so much about myself
and where i wanna go

i wanna go to drag race heaven
getting wheels everywhere

revvin' up at red lites, baby

when the dust settles i'll be there

tinker with the locket
it holds a sly surprise
puzzles—magic photographs
of me dressed in disguise

see—she pulls the curtain
royal as a queen
running in white linen gowns
awakened from a dream

there, he comes—a wild one
riding on Big Tim
and now they're flying fast upon
the clouds rolled out for them

the road stops at the castle
the room where she is cast
imprisoned by the dragon
this day to be her last

only had this one chance
she prayed that he would come

riding on that big white horse
and carrying the sun

oh, they tore the world apart
the dragon's deathly moans
echo thru the village as
the people all return home

he's a hero in a halo
she's a queen within a song
lovers in the quiet hours
holding tight until the dawn

all is well together
the lady and the man
how these tales are written
lovers take their stand

if you hold a dream
close inside your soul
and every day you feed it
it'll turn into your goal

and all the hopes you're promised
will sleep inside your eyes

if you love the sunlight
and travel thru her skies

tinker with the locket
it holds a story there
of all the dreams i've hidden
that grow beyond compare
into the flowers waving
to a world that can come true
it's all the love i'm giving
it all comes down to you...

what do you do with these pictures
i send on these pages so clean
are they a part of my diary somewhere
or are they the trash can's dream

one-way crush on you, boss-man
what is it like to be great
all of the girls in the hourglass
primped up in line at your gate

i've been working each day in a bank
and i'm leaving california this fall
a new mustang to lure me back homeward
my folks want me 'round when they call

so i'm going back home in october
time for a new road for me
and there won't be any messages for you
from inside my heartland—you'll see

i waited two years for a whisper
you never gave me any reply

and soon i'll go back to my southland
and wait for the boys to pass by

i'll become a teacher and daydream
about what it's like to be great
to have what you need at your doorstep
but then...that's not my fate

i'll never forget this affair
after two years. i've nothing to show
but chills and quick breaths and a heartbeat
whenever you're on my radio

my first love with a superstar—
well, baby.
is that all the luster you've got?
i'll take it all back in a harness
and go-ahead-on...ready or not

this is farewell to you
pen-pal
i know i'm a fool in your throng
remember that girl in your audience
hung up with your rock-'n-roll songs....

i'm gonna burn out
before i get thru
i'm gonna burn out, honey
waitin' out here for you.

my heart keeps achin'
overloaded at the end
am i just a fool for you
or am i gonna win

my shoes got holes
and my eyes are red
i stay this stoned
so i can see you in my head

my movin' rhythm's
done left me with the blues
'cause i'm 'bout to
burnout burnout burnout
payin' these lovesick dues

gonna burnout burnout
burnout before i'm done

gonna burnout burnout
'cause you're the only one
gonna burn burn burn
full speed straight ahead
gonna burnout burnout
alone in my bed

can't you see
that this woman needs her man
and not just any ole dude
she wants the one who understands
oh, lord, babee, can't you see
this lady's done got lost
she's burnedout burnedout
tryin' to locate The Boss

i'm gonna burnout
before i get thru
i'm gonna burnout, boss babee
what am i gonna do

my heart is achin'
my patience's wearin' thin
am i just another fool for you
or will my message sink in

and where are you now
my rock-'n-roll friend
what do you do
before the spotlights attend

do you go out to dinner
do you take in a show
do you sit at home
writing
long lists
when your things are slow

do you think of me too
doing laundry and food
do you wonder how i feel
as a hen with a brood

do you hold me up high
and let the light make her trace
and do you wonder what'll happen
when we're finally
there
face to face

i think about it.
i'm obsessed with your smell
altars and madmen
bound to my own little hell

everything sits out of focus
and nothing satisfies my soul
i move quickly in soft circles
playing havoc with the goal

have a nice summer
when's the new music release
will you play in my city
will the madness increase
will you know who i am
will you find me a place
or will i go home
taunt
with my windows erased...

he called me today
after months and months
and my sorrows
he called me
to see if i was still
this blue tomorrow

he was in cleveland
and i was here
and words were flipped around
like it hadn't been whole year

he called me today
doesn't matter, anymore
tho once there was a time
that i would have
gone thru the floor

got my mind on another
haven't met him yet
but he sings to me on the radio
he's the one
i don't forget

and millions of girls
stand in line for a chance
to see him
and touch him
be a part of his romance

what a situation
my mind and this guy
no matter where i put him
he's soon
back there in my eye

he sings and he sweats
and he screams out his pain
he's a downright sensation
and i'm a fool in this game

i belong to a legend
that everyone adores
and i'm waiting for a miracle
to send him
...right here...to my door....

sometimes i wonder
where it's all gonna lead
working a typewriter
my head racing full speed

drowning in music
between my ears
workin' a typewriter
my eyes filled with tears

factory music
rhymes on my tongue
man in the window
now, look what you've done

mother and mistress
wife and this whore
pacing the hourglass
begging for more

drums that keep beating
the clock and the song

waiting for someone
why does it take so long

the future is calling
her finger is curled
she's motioning toward me
as the music is whirled

playing recitals
all day in my head
working a typewriter
until it's been said

hear me, you
a'loose in your car
i'm counting these moments
as i sit in my jar

glass for my blue-sky
fluorescent sun
i know that you'll listen
before the year's done

within me sit rainbows
and children and hearts

within me sit thousands
of tears pulled apart

within me are diamonds
that glow in the dark
within me is a holocaust
as i sit here and bark

working a typewriter
it's just another day
listening to the music
playing...
so far away...

it seems like

i've been waiting

my whole lifetime

to find you

in a park

by the creek

but i'm left

as the assembly-line worker

with the newscasts

and the hourglass

every week

you are my soulmate

sweet visions

inspire

my fantasies

tonight

the winter's long shadow

makes me pale

and seem shallow

and i wonder

if i'll find you
in the light

true to my daydreams
and rainbows
filled with you
trembling
i wait
and what will i do
with your collection
on plastic

toe tap
sweet misery
at the gate

i belong to somebody
on the radio
and i pretend
in the darkness
he's near
and i close my eyes
inside his music

it's the tie
that binds me

right here....

i remember

being part of your audience

the first time

i saw you

arrive you

were smiling

thru all of the music

  —the actor

  displaying

  his jive....

and i sat

reposed

in your audience

boxed in

with my destiny, there

and i missed

the start

of my life-blood

as i watched

with a blank

empty stare

guy with the hat
the piano
musician
the artist
    —my dear
    what is this
    daydream
    within me
    and how can i
    make it
    come here

it's okay
to love a daydream
it's safe—
    i can read
    your soft lines

    on the paper
    in a store
    from your albums

    and turn them
    around
    'til they're mine

poor little girl
in the window
a baby
beside her today
and what
will she do
when the month
numbers two

    start over
    still lost
    in his sway....

ripped and riveted
can't you hear me call
still sending cheap letters
to a daydream
etched
on my wall....

you have your mountains
and cars
on the street
and hungry little girls
to fix
        all you can eat

and i
have this albatross
fast 'tween my teeth
unchartered passages
that turn bittersweet

soldier of angels
child to my breast

and another there, waiting
to return to my nest

i do these things
they seem silly, sometimes
writing to a rock-star
with my
        ordinary rhymes

i knew
that i'd find him
the man
for my time
from the way
that his thoughts
penned the words
next to mine

and i've been waiting
so long
that i hardly know what for
i've been waiting
alone
at the crossroads
and the door:

one-way march to heaven
one-way move to hell
the line that separates
the two
is a story i know well

is there restitution
is there home somewhere
is there anybody listening
doesn't anybody care?

probably
just a story
simple
—for a tune
as i break apart
and turn in anguish
from the whitewashed
        waiting-room

it is my father's house
and i will
satisfy him first
but will he recognize me

when my tears
begin to burst

it was
just a dream within me
it has
captured no reply
and where will i turn tomorrow
with this
angel
moving naked
in my eye....

this
is the end
of the scene:
        the actors
        have departed
        the star now
        takes the screen

possessed
—what is this thing
i've found?
someone
i love somewhere
someone
in the sound
someone
arched
inside my eye
and he's fast
leaving stardust
on my sigh

panic—

am i true

to my dream?

agony

am i foolish

as i scheme

whitewashed

at the mercy

of the deep

the star

begins to merge

and then he

loves me

in my sleep

waiting

with my toe-tap

on the ground

this

is the beginning

and this is some sweet

daydream

i have found....

i'm somebody's daughter
set off in the hills
waiting for good things
and baubles with thrills
i ain't got no weapons
feet to the ground
but i watch, look and listen
and then i gun down

this is some special party
i wonder what's lost
all my possessions
my 'good' name the cost
ain't got no home now
i wonder what's mine
only a mother
hangin' out on the line

preacher's revival
they call me a hoax
but my heart's on the table
carried by ghosts
you have your good times

eternity calls
i'm only a witness
caught up in the fall

tune up the music
in gabriel's key
beg, steal, and borrow
we come home to thee
sheep that are wayward
blood on the lamb
only the children
who got so out of hand

i have no future
i have no prime
i have no money
no friends left to bind
no peace enchanting
in the badlands i'm crossed
rumors of devils
the dice that get tossed

bring on the army
let the poor housewife be
quiet and humble

set out to be free
angels of fortune
i polish their wings
but i'm only a body
on the earth of a king

you can call me deceitful
i give in god's name
blasphemous cowgirl
her hands on the reins
gouge out my eyeballs
hollow my cheeks
nothing i care for
except what you seek....

I'm gonna write a book
about the things i've seen
to stand as a reminder
to the people
and the dream

the bible
turned your head around
captured
your debris
you hide behind
the words of old
and swear by god
you're free

one book
for our parents
one book
for the rest
one book
can change everything
    we visit
    with the guests

our father had a plan
unveiled a work of art
beautiful faces everywhere
and each one plays their part

you bring out the god
asleep within the seed
snatching souls
        from everywhere
        —the army
        and the need

turn in your lost shadows
i see them in a pile
the news is out—
he will return
among the rank-and-file

prophets of the angel world
now grace your hungry cry
to every mouth
a note of joy
is given
        in reply

the time has come
to organize
the world of rock-'n-roll
priests anointed
walk within
our chrome and glass
        fish bowl

salutations
greetings
        to the bright lights
        and the show
puppets
of the merry master
        bow
        and courtesy low

do you think it's true
are all my dreams
3-D
Or
am i just a soldier
shell-shocked
lost at sea

you supply the answer

our future's up to you

but i'll bet you even

jesus

would've

rock-'n-rolled

with the big boys, too....

don't be afraid

of the white horse with wings

he's only your beast

    of the times:

oft, i myself

had wished for the means

to leave this—

run home

    learn my lines

you say you're a dreamer

and you sympathize

with illusion

and nowhere to turn

i say

i'm the warrior

with arrows that sing

Wet

in the night

as I burn

puppet
the poet
preempted in crystal
i watch from
my place in the jar
        a move to the right
        with the hand and the pen
        and i know that i'm bound
        to a star

now resurrected
the father's new virgin
though her gowns
appear soiled
        from outside

        this is religion
        and this is survival
        springing a
        ferris-wheel ride

it comes down to slavery
the mentor looks painted
duties
of a gypsy undone

take out the weapons
defend my honor
for the battle's already
        begun

hear me:
selectors
of helmets and hemlines
while darning the sox
of a child
        this is forever
        abandoned in silence
        stroking me
        driving me
        wild

agent
pretender
adjusted and altered
resplendent
in solemn release
        dealer and gambler
        prisoner
        esthetic

causing the thin line
to cease

this is the rite
you can convince my journey
pull us together
as one

play your quick music
for you
are the martyr

into my father's
house come....

he had a '65 chevelle
and she had a factory block
boarded out to a 396
we'd race every weekend
at the local dragstrip
and then head out for
the drive-in flicks

we went together
for 5 years and then
we got married in my church
        wedding gown
and they polished up our hot rod
with cans and shoe paint
and we had a drag race
right across downtown

early american furniture
that 9-to-5 scene
and i bolted out when we split
to get straight
went off to college
sororities

i was normal
        but it was all too late

hooray, hooray
i'm a new-wave girl
tho i've grown a bit tight
at the seams
babies—bananas
and wild-flavored towns
my bellbottoms now
are pegged bluejeans

i watched it go down
from the southland's core
i was elated and relaxed with the style
then they laid the cards out
and said
        let's get with the truth
        and i
        blew them all away
        at the trial

i know i know
i'm a homegrown lass
wanna change all the things

that are wrong
but it ain't up to me
they keep it arranged
and all i do is wait
        and sing along

while y'awl were out there
groovin' and free
i was down
in the backstreets makin' time
with old folks and witches
they were brewing up a scheme
to steep it up and make it all shine

i don't have the money
i don't have the inside-line
and i don't have a home and family
but i see the buzzards up there
circlin' the sky
and i know that it's time to get free

help me, somebody
get in touch with my hands
and we'll join in the windows
for the show

of puppets and players
and honkey-tonk bars
all the strangers are ready to go

tonite tonite
the highway dead-ends
i'm gonna take to the streets
in the sky
'cause that's all that's left
with pollution controls
gonna wipe 'em out as i fly by

raise hell
raise your flag
raise your hand
in the count
are you with me
are you
          out on the line
crusin'
in fourth gear
got the windows rolled down
and springsteen's on the tape
soundin' fine

a dream
a wish
a preposterous idea
but
who else asked the angels
for the key
while y'awl were busy
with fortunes and guitars
i settled for the exclusive recipe

esoteric

exitonic

neon exxon sign

is that the sun

shinin' thru there in the night

or

am i a fool

doin' wheelies downtown

and revvin' up at every red light

today today

i would love to sit back

in a house with a man who stays home

but

i throw the horse shoes

and gamble just a bit

i can wait

to greet tomorrow

on my own....

i've been
waiting for you
for a year
if i told
my old friends
they'd say
i'm not thinking
too clear

yet it
makes sense to me
(but just me, alone)
i live
in white boxes
wishing
and wishing
for the bone

is there
space for a heartbeat
beside you at night
one just like yours
thumping

with the
        flashing green light

i know who i am
i've got
engines and toys
i know what there is
between all of us boys
i know there's a future
a man for my time
i know
that he's waiting
at the crossroads
and the sign

is there
sorrow
in the faces
that turn to you
for soul—
is there pain
in the meetings
that make you
realize
        they've grown old

a journey so simple
from here
out to there
but it takes
a whole lifetime
to show
        how much you care

do you care
'bout the days
as they stretch
for your heart
or the dogs
and the harnesses
as they
        take you apart

or the women
with the cameras
an eye in repose
the plates
are never empty
in the rooms
where you go

is there
anything waiting
for you to complete—
a room
with white music
and toes
that tap
        to the beat...

is there
something you need?
i'll just
ease out this door—
it's windy
this daybreak
time to
        try it once more...

it seems like

i've been waiting

my whole lifetime

to find you

    in a park

    by the creek

    but i'm left

    the assembly-line worker

    with the newscasts

    and the hourglass

    every week

you are my soulmate

sweet visions

inspire

my fantasies

tonight

    winter's long shadow

    makes me pale

    and seem shallow

and i wonder
if i'll find you
in the light

true to my daydreams
and rainbows
filled with you
trembling
i wait

and what
will i do
with your collection
on plastic

toe-tap
sweet misery
at the gate

i belong to somebody
on the radio
and i pretend in the darkness
he's near
and i close my eyes

inside his music

it's the tie that

binds me

        right here

i woke up

alone

in the dawn

and i could hear them

making love

downstairs

        apartment dwellers

        are such brave souls

always

so exposed and bare

nothing

but the jewels

to haunt me as a friend

nothing

but somebody's love

will make me smile

        now that I've reached

        another end

mistrustful

undaunted

        so cute on the cross

with an attitude for strangers
and everything i've lost

woe-begotten
step aside
this is my fate—ascend
i woke alone
and winter is coming
and i refuse
to let the darkness in

empty
alone
as just i can be
where is somebody
who will alter me

feed me to the meadows
tear me with the tide
hold me open soft at night
and let me stretch out wide

i've grown long and thin
my body aches again

and i never feel emergencies
arise
yet i'm caught out—there
a wayward drum that snares
and i wonder
why it hurts me
        this disguise

dear god, i'm yours
and your music
full of cures
and no one can accomplish
        in your place

        for
        in the tunnels uptown
        my body falls to the ground
        groping
        in the darkness
        for someplace

        a place to just kneel down
        a place to wash this gown
        a place to put these bundles
        'til i leave

just another heart
another actor
plays the part
abandoned
in the shadows:
yes, i believe.

and a girl gone wild
an old and weary child
who calls you
can you hear me
when i grieve

oh, baby, won't ya give me a ride
i'm so downhome lonely
and i need a place to hide
obscure and overdue
roaches in my shoes!
a shower and a bed
        i got the bus station blues

if you've got some pennies
i got a little time
i can tell your fortune
you can have a hunk of mine
and if you got a hankerin'
and nothin' else to lose
let's get down
        I got the bus-station blues

i'd trade the ring that
my sweet love gave
if you'd cuddle up with me
and make myself behave
i'm a good woman, really,
lived my life in twos—

all alone and waitin' with
    my bus-station blues

well, i got a game
i can teach you mystery
and i got some, honey
saved for you and me
if you like my flowers
and you need a clue:
take off your jeans
    i got the bus-station blues...

her windswept ways
are a tantalizing come-on
she lives inside a box
and her old man's got a gun-on
if you're lookin' for a lover
and she's got you on a line
better take her down
'cause she would
make you feel so fine....

pickin' up my long gown
payin' all my dues
measuring the cost
by the handiwork of fools
i'm the one you want tonight
'cause i know i want you, too
strung out on some honky-tonk
the lady with the blues....

the flowers i grow
in the window by the sea
lean into my light
when i'm feelin' kinda free

and i pick up my petticoats
down in the sand
to a lazy banjo pluckin' out
the music in my hand

pickin' up my long gown
waitin' for a cue
to stop you on the highway
get it with the mornin' dew
i'm the one you want beside you
'cause you know i want you, too
strung out on some honky-tonk
the lady with the blues....

well, i'm an angel bound for heaven
with the white clouds for my dress
i'm the woman knelt before you
tryin' to confess
i'm the hustler at the bus stop
beggin' for a chance
to wile away the night
with the music and a dance....

pickin' up my long gown
throw away my shoes

got a movin' rhythm

and you can have it, too

just reach out and touch me, honey

love is always new

strung out on some honky-tonkin'

lady with the blues....

I.

i was standing across
crystal bridges, so lost
reaching up
'neath the sun
calling softly
when my words
fell upon
your blind ears
they were gone
leaving memories
still traced
in your laughter;
then the nearness of you
washed my soul
as the dew
sustains all of its seed
for the master....

II.

i can't tell you
how long

it has been
since a smile
and a song
thundered out
of my shadow;
in the moon
i have seen
promises of a dream
i've been waiting
with laurels
of thanksgiving;
it will come
as a dove
white and clean
full of love
flying free
with a light
for the living....

III.

if you wonder
how far
you can see
through my jar

oh, the glass
of illusion
reflects you;
i have come
of the earth
mortal man
gave me birth
but my spirit
is woven around you.
and there will
be the times
crowded rooms
waiting lines
when you'll stand
raise your hand
and you'll know it;
for the truth
lies within
armored sparks
for the men
clothed in greetings
of angels
for the prophet.

IV.

then we'll lie
by the sea
making love
feeling free
and we'll find, then,
a reason
for the sowing;
for a seed
is a star
watered long
leaning far
we'll rise up, watch
our love-music growing.
and by the judge
we'll kneel down
painted hands
thorny crown
we are close
to a quake of the sunrise....

i can

waste this day

but not another lonely play

not another night

with the echoes

from downstairs

not another town that's new

not another darkness—view

not another dream

misplaced

among the flares

baby, i know you're out there

have ya got a dime to spare

will ya call me

anything

give me a ride

'cause i'm new in town

and i wanna

get around

these walls

that lock me
from outside

and if you'll hold me
then
i think that i can
smile again
and then
the night would greet me
with a key

to unlock a door
and then you can
put it to the floor
if you'll just slow down
in second
for the curve

'cause i'm a brazen horse
and i will run this course
but i need someone
to catch me
when i swerve

and i know about the gears
and i've put it
thru the tears
and it's all that i amount to
    yesterday

    a drag-styled queen
    waitin' for somebody's
    limousine
    comin'
    for to carry her away

    and i have tried so hard
    the reckless
    soul-food bard

    maybe
    you'll step in
    to save the day...

it's been a bleak asylum
it's been a faulty measure
counting the ways to make you
admit there's more to pleasure

i did not know the meaning
it was the resolutions
i lost my countenance
i held some substitutions

you led me to remember
opened the entertainer
awoke my breasts and beaches
courting the window-maker

you left me in a frenzy
i have no place to alter
reborn in destitution
silk gowns that shake and falter

this is my sentence-warrior
rendezvous of the haunted

you give me full salvation
all that i ever wanted

can you accept a martyr
can you adore the center
it grows on blood and sorrow
if only you will enter

you'll find the heaven rendered
you'll find it in our passion
a love on nails and pillows
a master of compassion

the bruce poems

patti

#0

i hear your voices calling
amid the ghosts of daybreak
and then i see the future
straddle the fool within me

i am your closet hoodlum
who stalks your sleep with starlight
born of the white illusion
tormenting your desire

we can begin together
i give you center stage
if you will help me dazzle
potential deep within me

you asked me for your father
you asked for energy
i bring you the new religion
torn from the flames
that set me free....

the bruce poems
#1

i saw you
last night in my dream
    your face
    it was shinin'
    with light
    and even
    your hair
    looked golden

    and i knew
    that you loved me
    last night

it goes
a bit further
than fortunes
it runs
a bit faster
than sound

and it comes
from a place
in my heart-land
    i'm in love
    with a man
    who's spellbound

you played your guitar
to me tuesday
we were one
and suspended
in the crowd

    i never knew a man
    existed like you
    and now it makes me
        feel so proud

young man
you are blocked from me
somewhere
    coat and ties
    truck drivers
    valets

no one
seems to care
'bout my heart-land
no one
would let me pass into
your play

it was a stock
13.8 in the quarter
foot hoppin'
for the green light
to turn

and the rubber
and the race
sent me flyin'
into
those fires that burn

i saw you
last night
you were smiling
i wanna give you
a boy
that's your own

i wanna give you
all the strings
to my heart-land

second gear
in the curve
get me home....

the bruce poems
#2

i woke up
alone
in the dawn
and i could hear them
making love
downstairs

    apartment dwellers
    are such brave souls:
    always
    so exposed and bare

nothing
but the jewels
to haunt me as a friend
nothing
but somebody's love
will make me smile
    now that i've reached
    another end

mistrustful
undaunted
    so cute on the cross
    with an attitude for strangers
    and everything i've lost

woe begotten
step aside
this is my fate
    ascent

    i woke alone
    and winter is coming
    and i refuse
    to let the darkness in

empty
alone
as just i can be
where is somebody
who will alter-me

    feed me to the meadows
    tear me with the tide

hold me open soft at night
and let me stretch out wide

i've grown long and thin
my body aches again
and i never feel emergencies
arise
yet i'm caught out there
a wayward drum that snares
and i wonder
why it hurts me
this disguise

dear god, i'm yours
and your music
full of cures
and no one can accomplish
in your place

for
in the tunnels uptown
my body falls to the ground
groping
in the darkness
for someplace

a place to just kneel down
a place to wash this gown
a place to put these bundles
'til i leave

just another heart
another actor
plays the part
abandoned
in the shadows:
yes, i believe.

and a girl gone wild
an old and weary child
who calls you
can you hear me
when i grieve

i can
waste this day
but not another lonely play
not another night
with the echoes
from downstairs

not another town that's new
not another darkness-view
not another dream
        misplaced
        among the flares

baby, i know you're out there
have ya got a dime to spare
        will ya call me
        anything
        give me a ride

        'cause i'm new in town
        and i wanna
        get around
        these walls
        that lock me
        from outside

and if you'll hold me
then
i think that i can
smile again
and then

the night would greet me
with a key

to unlock a door
and then you can
put it to the floor
if you'll just slow down
in second
for the curve

'cause i'm a brazen horse
and i will run this course
but i need someone
to catch me
when i swerve

and i know about the gears
and i've put it
thru the tears
and it's all
that i amount to
        yesterday

a drag-styled queen
waitin' for somebody's

limousine
comin'
for to carry her away

and i have tried so hard
the reckless
soul-food bard

maybe
you'll step in
to save the day....

the bruce poems
#3

i made
thru another night
alone
        you might ask yourself
        is this person
        overblown?

a night without
love
in the quiet
a night without
murmurs
        it's lost
a night
alone
in the darkness
        makes me still
        with the cost

i lived in the forests
as my life

and the play
was what kept me
 aside

 and i saw
 sweet things
 like no other
 and then it
 took me for a ride

turned upside-down
and the hourglass
caught up
in the time
as it ran
and i
begged for release
from the harness
 and they told me,
 look
 for a man.

instructions
in love
and i studied
became

a wild tender
of hearts
        and i took
        what was sent
        from the darkness
        and
        i got torn apart.

i remember
the horse
flying with me
the mornings
        i dared to unwind
        all the love
        on my heart-strings
        and
        it made me kind

i worship
the natural beauty
i find it
in windy white skies

        and i find it
        tucked in clear windows

of
my lover's eyes

love:
its expression
anoints me
a sacrament
yes, i can go

but i run away
to the white-skies
and
it makes me glow

a master of fires
you take me
to the world
that reflects my lost peace
and often
i escape
in your thunder
and
i get some release....

I saw you
last night in my dream
your face
it was shinin'
with light
and you
and even your hair
looked golden
and I know
that you loved me
last night…

it goes
a lot further
than fortunes
it runs
a bit taste
than sound
and it comes
from a place
in my heart-land
I'm in love

With a man
Who's spellbound

You played
Your guitar
To me Tuesday
At one
And suspended
In the crowd

I never knew a man
Existed like you
And now it makes me
Feel so proud

Young man
You are blocked from me
It was A-stock
13.8 in the guitar
foot hoppin'
for the green light
to turn
and the rubber
and the race
sent me flyin'

into

these fires that burn

I saw you

last night

you were smiling

i wanna give you

a boy

that's your own

i wanna give you

all the strings

to my heart-land

second gear

in the curve

get me home.

you were
such a sexy lover
you know
there couldn't be another

why are you
telling me it's over
where's my dreams:
    you say
    some organization's
    gonna
    stop this sweet relation
    and you're
    tearing me across
    the empty screens

remember me, baby
how you
make me get crazy
    overloaded
    and taunt
    in my jeans

it took me so long
        to steady myself
and the splendor
        of your loving
        turned me 'round

        i can
        feel you so close
        you're a
        fairytale ghost

        now
        you say you're gonna take me
        down

been feeling so sick
        all the time
you shouldn't
        love southern girls
        who make you soft rhymes

        i wish
        i had more
        or maybe less
        the things

that you showed me
have made me a mess....

do i turn
in the streetlights
and sigh
do i take
someone's arm
and show him
your harm
or wait
with my sad lullaby....

won't you
send me
your wild
limousines....

CPSIA information can be obtained
at www.ICGtesting.com
Printed in the USA
LVHW070836050123
736515LV00001B/1